AMERICAN PROFILES

GREAT WOMEN WRITERS
1900–1950

■

Christina Gombar

Facts On File, Inc.
AN INFOBASE HOLDINGS COMPANY

Great WomenWriters 1900–1950

Facts On File, Inc.
11 Penn Plaza
New York, NY 10001

Library of Congress Cataloging-in-Publication Data
Gombar, Christina.
   Great women writers, 1900–1950 / Christina Gombar.
       p.   cm. — (American profiles)
   Includes bibliographical references and index.
   Contents: Edith Wharton: America's social critic — Willa Cather: novelist of the Great Frontier — Gertrude Stein: the great innovator — Katherine Anne Porter: "It all happened" — Zora Neale Hurston: genius of the South — Pearl Buck: writer of two worlds — Eudora Welty: capturing the still moment — Flannery O'Connor: writer of violence and vision.
   ISBN 0-8160-3060-X
   1. Women authors, American—20th century—Biography—Juvenile literature. [1. American literature—Women authors. 2. Authors, American. 3. Women—Biography.] I. Title. II. Series: American profiles (Facts On File, Inc.)
PS151.G56   1996
810.9'9287—dc20
[B]   95-43305

Cover design by Matt Galemmo

This book is printed on acid-free paper.

Printed in the United States of America

MP FOF 10 9 8 7 6 5 4 3 2 1

Contents

Acknowledgments

I would like to thank The Goodman Fund of the City University of New York and the New York Foundation for the Arts for their financial assistance in the completion of this book. I thank my husband and my family for their support and patience. For their guidance and inspiration, I would like to thank Dr. Leo Hamalian, Dr. Laura Hinton, and Linsey Abrams, of the City University of New York.

Thanks also to James Warren, for his help and editorial direction in shaping the idea that became the book, and to my editor, Jeffrey Golick, who saw the idea to its completion.

Introduction

*T*he period of literary history covered in this book, roughly 1900 to 1950, was a time of unprecedented change—for the world at large, for America, and particularly for women.

In 1862, when Edith Wharton was born, America was less than a century old; a woman's place was in the kitchen, not at a writing desk or in the workplace; and women's right to vote was several decades away. At the turn of the century, in fact, women had almost no rights under the law—but across America they were plowing fields, helping to complete the settling of the West and the rebuilding of the South. Some—among them Gertrude Stein and Willa Cather—were even attending college. As the twentieth century advanced, many more broke into careers that had previously been closed to them, not the least of which was writing.

In the nineteenth century and before, the few women writers who did publish books had often been criticized for their narrow range of subject matter; typically the main theme of women's fiction was romance. During this century, as women took on a greater variety of roles in society, the literature they produced was thereby enriched. They portrayed a wide range of American experiences—from the hypocrisy of upper-class drawing rooms in New York, to the devastation of the South in the aftermath of the Civil War, to the rigors of the Western frontier, to the turbulence of Europe and the Far East during times of political change.

All of the women profiled in this collection achieved literary distinction against considerable odds. Edith Wharton faced down the disapproval of her family, struggled with depression, and suffered several nervous breakdowns before emerging as one of the century's greatest American authors. Others, like Zora Neale Hurston and Katherine Anne Porter, were abandoned children, who produced great literature as part of a struggle for survival; Flannery O'Connor fought against time and a lethal illness to produce an unforgettable body of work.

Writers' lives are never easy. They stand outside mainstream society, toiling with no guarantee of recognition or financial reward. A woman writer's life is perhaps doubly difficult. Writing earlier in this century, English author Virginia Woolf addressed the question "Why aren't there more great women writers?" in her essay *A Room of One's Own.* She concluded that the main reasons women were not allowed to become great writers were family opposition, lack of education, and poverty. There were two reasons for the poverty: first, because of inheritance laws, money was passed from fathers to sons; and second, women produced children, which prevented them from having the time to either earn their own money or create their own literature.

Among the authors discussed here, those who had independent means to support their writing, such as Edith Wharton and Gertrude Stein, had a somewhat easier time of it. Others benefited from the changing times, pursuing auxiliary careers. Willa Cather, Katherine Anne Porter, Zora Neale Hurston, and Eudora Welty were all journalists; Pearl Buck worked as a missionary and a college teacher. It is interesting to note that those with the grimmest beginnings, such as Hurston, produced the most uplifting literature, while the most financially fortunate of the group—Wharton—produced some of the darkest tales in American literature.

None of these women was "typical" for her time. The earliest of these writers chafed at the societal constraints placed on both women and writers in America. Some dealt with the situation by becoming permanent expatriates, while others lived for long stretches overseas, savoring the freedom and enriched perspective that living abroad gave them. Only Pearl Buck had children, and only she could claim a happy and long-lasting marriage. Not one woman was supported in her writing career by the financial help of her husband.

Many of these authors did not achieve literary recognition until they had reached middle age. Their long years of effort, often in the face of initial public and critical failure, spurred these writers to greater achievements and brought forth their best work.

In the process of struggling to find their own voices, these American women writers evolved new ways of telling stories that have greatly enriched the American literary tradition. Gertrude Stein, Willa Cather, and Eudora Welty are all noted for devising fresh ways of storytelling that make their fiction seem very close to life as it is actually experienced.

Though many of these authors' books have suspenseful plots, their works also display a richly poetic style, and feature truthful depictions of emotion, human relationships, and society and family life. Their strength is often in bringing meaning to the simple situations and everyday lives of ordinary people.

These women wrote on themes of love, social progress, personal morality, and religious redemption. Some of them, like Edith Wharton, directly addressed concerns that were specific to women, such as their limited role in society. Others, like Cather and Porter, portrayed women whom the authors had known in their own lives—women who were leaders and adventurers.

The works of these authors can also be read as history, since they describe women's roles in settling the frontier, in keeping families and society going in the post–Civil War South, and in raising their families, beginning with Edith Wharton a full century ago.

Like all great art, the stories and novels of these authors raise timeless questions. Katherine Anne Porter can show us that long before Viet Nam, Americans were ambivalent about fighting a war abroad. Willa Cather wrote of the difficulties faced by immigrants who, hoping to find a better life in America, were faced with overwhelming hardships. Zora Neale Hurston captured a rapidly disappearing African-American folk culture; her writing raises questions about racial identity that are still pertinent today. Flannery O'Connor explored the particularly American phenomenon of violence, searching for some redeeming meaning behind it. Pearl Buck wrote of Far Eastern culture at a time when most Americans thought it not worth serious consideration; recognizing the dangers of trying to "westernize" the East, she advised Americans to listen to and learn from other cultures. This advice seems especially prescient today, when the idea of a global village is fast becoming a reality.

In an age when films and television and even much popular literature offer a superficial view of people, these works offer a view of life in all its ambiguity and complexity. This book attempts to enrich readers' experience of these works by providing some insight into the authors' lives. All of the writers whose works are examined here are outstanding—for their contributions to the American literary tradition, for possessing originality and vision that continue to influence writers of today, and for having had the courage to make their voices heard.

Edith Wharton
America's Social Critic

Though she appeared every inch the upper-class lady she was raised to be, Edith Wharton was unhappy in the role of society wife. Her unfulfilled literary aspirations contributed to the nervous breakdowns she suffered as a young wife; she eventually achieved success as a writer in middle age, becoming the first woman to win the coveted Pulitzer Prize.
(Library of Congress)

*I*n 1873, eleven-year-old Edith Jones presented her mother with her first attempt at a novel. It began:

"Oh, how do you do, Mrs. Brown?" said Mrs. Tompkins. "If only I had known you were going to call I should have tidied up the drawing room."

1

Edith's mother handed the manuscript back to her daughter. "Drawing rooms," she stated coldly, "are *always* tidy." She refused to read on.

Thus began a characteristic pattern in the fledgling writer's career. All her life, the young girl who would become the great writer Edith Wharton would set down her honest assessments of what she observed in American society. Her depictions frequently embarrassed or offended the segment of society she scrutinized, and the writer would be censured for her efforts.

Edith Wharton wrote during the pivotal decades following the turn of the century, and her fiction depicts characters who reflect a changing American society. During the author's lifetime, both her native New York City and America at large were radically transfigured by the booming commercialism that followed the Civil War. A country founded on Puritan values and based on a farming economy burgeoned into an industrial, westward-expanding nation focused on commerce, speculation, and the pursuit of ever-greater wealth and material opulence.

The new leaders of America's "Gilded Age" of the 1890s and early 1900s discarded the pieties and conservative strictures of old, staid, and powerful New York families like the one the author had been born into. Over the course of her literary lifetime, Wharton would lampoon the follies of the new rich and sharply critique the stifling conservatism of the old society. In her work, she would repeatedly link the greed and exploitation that characterized the new materialist America with the waste and abuse of human spirit and potential.

Edith Wharton was born Edith Newbold Jones in New York City on January 24, 1862, the third of three children and the only girl in the family. Both of Edith's parents came from distinguished old American families. Edith's maternal great-grandfather, General Ebenezer Stevens, was a Revolutionary War hero. Edith's father, George Jones, had sufficient inherited wealth that he never needed to work for a living.

Edith's mother, Lucretia Jones, was preoccupied with spending lavishly on clothes and entertainment, and left Edith's care largely to household servants. All her life, the writer would have a cool and distant relationship with her mother. Fortunately, she enjoyed closer and more affectionate ties with her father. George Jones was a man of culture, and his West Twenty-third Street brownstone boasted a considerable library, a favorite spot for little Edith. Long before she learned her alphabet, she would walk up and down the length of this library, an open book in hand, pretending to read aloud, or "making up," as she called her early fabrications. Her brothers Harry and Frederic were, respectively, twelve and sixteen years her senior, and when Edith was little more than a toddler, they were being prepared for college at home by a young English tutor. Little Edith would sneak into their schoolroom and play quietly in a corner while the tutor read Greek mythology and the great works of poetry aloud to his students. No doubt her "making up" was inspired by his example.

In 1866, when the United States was slumped in a severe recession following the Civil War, the Joneses leased out their New York home and set off for Europe. They dropped their younger son, Harry, off at Cambridge University in England—Frederic was at Harvard—and began a leisurely six-year journey across the Continent. The years of exposure to European culture had an indelible effect on Edith—the great cathedrals, palaces, and ancient ruins fired her curiosity and creative imagination.

Edith was educated haphazardly during her years in Europe. On her return to America at age ten, she delved freely into her father's library, consuming the classics—Chaucer, Shakespeare, and Greek mythology—along with the works of the American writers Washington Irving and Henry Wadsworth Longfellow. When a young German woman was hired as her tutor, she introduced Edith to the works of the German author Goethe and to the new German philosophies—not usual areas of study for girls.

Soon Edith was attempting to compose her own stories, but she was relentlessly critical of the products of her efforts. She even fabricated amusingly scathing reviews of her work. Of her first novella, written at thirteen, she wrote, "Every character is a failure, the plot a vacuum, the style spiritless, the dialogue vague, the sentiment weak and the whole thing a fiasco."

When she was fourteen, her brother Harry—the only family member who encouraged her writing—arranged to have some of her poems published anonymously in the *Atlantic Monthly* magazine. Two years later, he paid to have a collection of her poems published privately.

Up to now, Edith's parents had indulged her in her intellectual pursuits. But as she approached a marriageable age, they took a firm stand against her writing. Her duty in life, they said, was not to write books, but to emulate her mother's career of family, leisure, and entertaining. This would only be possible if she married.

At twenty, Edith was taken up by New York's fashionable young married set. At their dinner tables, her quick mind and witty conversation were valued as much as her stylish appearance.

It was in this milieu that Edith met Edward "Teddy" Wharton. In him Edith sensed a cheerful and tolerant soul. Though he was not an intellectual like her, he loved to travel, and more important, he had no objections to her literary ambitions. Edith's marriage to Wharton in 1885 freed her from her mother's domination, brought her a share of her inheritance, and opened the door to further travel to her beloved Europe.

Immediately upon returning from a long wedding trip, Wharton began sending out her poetry for publication, and was overjoyed when some of her verses were accepted by *Harper's* magazine. Although absorbed in running two households (one in New York and one in Newport, Rhode Island) and traveling with her husband, Wharton continued to write steadily. Her social status gave her access to authors like the French novelist Paul Bourget and the American expatriate Henry James, who became her good friend and encouraged her to submit her short stories for publication. But for several years her pieces were rejected as often as they were published. Stories like "The Bunner Sisters," about two women swindled into destitution after one marries a fiendish man, were too depressing, editors said. Publishers were looking for upbeat stories, reflecting the high hopes of America's prosperous Gilded Age. But Wharton's concerns lay elsewhere. The American dream of independence and freedom, she felt, did not extend to women.

Her 1894 story "The Valley of Childish Things" depicted men who were not ready to accept intelligent, independent-thinking, mature women. While other writers ended their novels with marriage as an equation for happiness, Wharton used marriage as a starting point, and went on to expose the limitations of the institution as she had observed it in society and in her own life.

For Wharton's marriage had proved to be a disappointment. Her marriage had failed to provide the passionate love she had anticipated, and as time went on, she felt more and more keenly the lack of shared intellectual interests with her husband. Moreover, the Whartons had no children; this grew to be Edith's greatest sorrow in life. This unhappiness, combined with her faltering writing career, contributed to the series of nervous breakdowns Wharton suffered as she entered her mid-thirties. A doctor advised her to use her writing as therapy, and it turned out to be a successful strategy. When she emerged from her depression, she had acquired the detachment necessary for effective writing, and now she faced her work with new determination and focus.

In 1899, Wharton's first short-story collection, *The Greater Inclination*, was published by Scribner's, a leading New York publisher. The book marked the beginning of a period of extraordinary confidence and productivity. Three novels followed in quick succession: *The Touchstone* (1900), *The Valley of Decision* (1902), and *Sanctuary* (1903). These early works garnered mixed but encouraging reviews from critics, who most frequently compared her style to that of Henry James, who, like her, wrote of upper-class Americans, often against a European backdrop.

It wasn't until *The House of Mirth*, published in 1905, that Wharton finally triumphed in conveying a portrait of thwarted womanhood that was both subtle and moving.

The novel depicts the last eighteen months in the life of Lily Bart, a beautiful young woman who had been raised in wealth but was suddenly plunged into poverty following her father's financial failure and the subsequent deaths of both her parents.

Lily's entire upbringing had prepared her for no other career than that of society wife. She was extraordinarily beautiful and refined; an admiring character observing her "had a confused sense that she must have cost a great deal to make, that a great many dull and ugly people must . . . have been sacrificed to produce her."

At the story's outset, Lily understands that her charm, breeding, and sex appeal could gain her a rich husband, who would value her purely as a possession. But she cannot quite accept this role, and bungles every would-be match. She hangs on to the fringes of society, first living with a straightlaced old aunt who eventually disinherits her for the "grave sins" of smoking and running up debts at bridge. Lily next serves as a private social secretary for her best friend, an older, *nouveau riche* married woman, but is quickly dropped after the woman's husband makes advances toward her.

Although misguided, Lily does have some sympathetic qualities. After a run of luck on the stock market, she impulsively donates a generous sum to a hostel for sick and impoverished young working women, and she visits their living quarters. But at thirty, her ornamental value is waning and her marriage prospects have plummeted. Lily tries work in a hat shop, fails, and eventually sinks to a seedy boarding house existence. Demoralized, she eloquently articulates her plight:

> *"I have tried hard, but life is difficult, and I am a very useless person. I can hardly be said to have an independent existence. I was just a screw or a cog in the great machine I called life, and when I dropped out of it I found I was of no use anywhere . . . What can one do when one finds that one only fits into one hole? One must get back to it or be thrown out in the rubbish heap—and you don't know what it's like in the rubbish heap!"*

Lily has one last chance to save herself, but the plan would require blackmailing a friend. She chooses loyalty to the friend over financial salvation, and dies of an accidental drug overdose, forgotten by the society that has destroyed her.

The House of Mirth targets both the "old" New York for its intolerance and the "new money" for its heartlessness. It is a merciless portrait of a society bereft of the values Wharton herself most cherished—loyalty, empathy, charity, and family feeling.

Critics complained that the frivolous Lily was not an appropriate heroine. But so compassionate was Wharton's depiction of her plight that readers were inevitably won over to the heroine's point of view. *The House of Mirth* was an immediate best-seller. The public enjoyed its scandalous glimpse into the fashionable society Wharton knew well. The people most scathingly indicted were not of her own ancient stock but of the newly monied, pleasure-seeking class. The book's title comes from the book of Ecclesiastes in the Old Testament: "The heart of the wise is in the house of mourning, but the heart of fools is in the house of mirth."

In 1901, Wharton sold her Newport, Rhode Island, cottage and built a new home called The Mount, in Lenox, Massachusetts, a rural town in the heart of the Berkshire mountains. Her next novel, *The Fruit of the Tree*, published in 1907, was set in this region, and incorporated an exposé of industrial working conditions in Lenox-area mills, a discussion of euthanasia—or mercy killing—and a further critique of marriage. While *The House of Mirth* showed the consequences of failing to marry, *The Fruit of the Tree* showed that even the most enlightened husband could turn oppressive. The book depicts a marriage in which a man, remarrying after being widowed, at first accepts his liberated second wife, but later rejects her, preferring to worship a false image of his spoiled, childish first wife.

Edith Wharton was by now a commercially successful and critically acclaimed author. She was often compared with George Eliot, the great British woman novelist who also wrote of individual moral dilemmas played out against a broad social canvas. Wharton's short stories—often spare, chilling, and pessimistic—drew comparisons with those of Nathaniel Hawthorne, whose work she greatly admired.

Although extremely prolific during the first decade of the century—she published several books on home decorating and gardening, as well as poetry and prose—Wharton maintained an active social life. She rose at six each morning and wrote in bed for several hours, peeling off her handwritten manuscript pages for her secretary—her former German tutor—to type. By noon she would appear in her drawing room, perfectly coiffed and turned out to greet her guests. She was at times almost manic in her productivity, and would work herself to the point of exhaustion, then succumb to a period of enforced rest before returning to her demanding schedule.

In the first decade of the century, Wharton began to spend part of each year in Paris. She felt comfortable in France, where society allowed a greater latitude in lifestyles, and artists and intellectuals enjoyed an esteem and social position that compared favorably with their relatively low status in America. From Paris, she took frequent trips to England to visit her friend Henry James. Through James, she met Morton Fullerton, a brilliant American journalist then working as the Paris correspondent for the London *Times*.

By the time Wharton met Fullerton, she and Teddy had been having marital troubles for some years. The couple had lived on Edith's inherited wealth, which was later supplemented by her impressive literary earnings. This, added to Edith's new fame, caused tension, and the couple often lived separately.

Wharton began a relationship with Fullerton in 1907. She was forty-five, he three years younger. Fullerton was a renowned ladies' man, and had no desire to settle down permanently with Wharton. Their liaison ended after three years, and the two remained friends.

The affair with Morton Fullerton marked the first time the author had fallen passionately in love. Her subsequent disillusionment inevitably found expression in her writing. In

1911, she published her best-known work, *Ethan Frome*, a short novel of relentlessly morbid suspense.

Set among the rural poor in an area much like Lenox, Massachusetts, *Ethan Frome* is the story of a young man unhappily married to a witchlike older woman. He falls in love with his wife's young cousin, an orphaned young woman named Mattie Silver, who has been living and working in his farmhouse for a year. When Zeena, his wife, learns of their love, she orders the penniless girl away. Neither Ethan nor Mattie can bear the thought of a future without each other.

Ethan has considered running away with Mattie, but a sense of duty toward his wife has restrained him. They set out for the train station where they are to part forever, but before reaching there the would-be lovers stop for one spurious pleasure: a wild, mile-long ride on a sled through the crisp night. After the ride is over, Mattie makes a proposal to Ethan: that instead of continuing their journey to the train station and their separate fates, they take another sled ride—but this time, the ride will end with their joint suicide as they deliberately crash the sled into a tree. Ethan at first protests, then remounts the sled, and the two set off on their disastrous night ride.

But Mattie's plan fails. They crash into the tree, but instead of finding blissful oblivion, Ethan slowly comes to consciousness:

> *The stillness was so profound that he heard a little animal twittering somewhere near by under the snow . . . that made a small frightened cheep like a field mouse . . . he understood that it must be in pain; pain so excruciating that he seemed, mysteriously, to feel it shooting through his own body . . . The thought of the animal's suffering was intolerable to him and he struggled to raise himself, and could not because a rock, or some huge mass, seemed to be lying on him.*

Ethan emerges from the crash maimed and permanently hunched over. Mattie, the source of the frightened animal noise in the snow, is paralyzed. The reader next sees the cast of characters living miserably together more than twenty years in the future, when Mattie and Ethan's wife Zeena are almost indistinguishable.

Wharton found the relaxed and libertarian atmosphere of Paris a better environment for writing than her native New York City. She spent the last several decades of her life in France, writing happily and prolifically, and there she wrote the Pulitzer Prize–winning novel The Age of Innocence, *a bittersweet look at the conservative nineteenth-century New York society in which she had grown up.*
(Library of Congress)

Ethan Frome shatters the myth of romantic love, while painting a heartrending portrait of human emotional cravings at war with social duty. It was a struggle close to Edith's own heart. Although long unhappy in her marriage, Edith had fundamental moral objections to divorce, and scorned the easy formation of new marital ties. *Ethan Frome* was published during a period of great turmoil in the author's life. While Edith had been living for long stretches in Paris, her husband had been having an affair. Around this time, he confessed both to the affair and to having speculated and lost some $10,000 of Edith's money, which she had always trusted him to manage. Her husband paid back the money with a timely inheritance, but the Whartons seldom lived together after the incident, and divorced in 1913. Teddy spent his old age careening around Europe, drunk, usually with several young women in tow. In 1911 Edith had sold The Mount, and by 1913, Paris was her permanent home. America, nonetheless, remained her primary literary focus.

Her controversial 1913 novel, *The Custom of the Country*, charted the career of an American woman who made a business of marriage. The heroine, Undine Spragg, took for granted that each of her husbands valued her only as decorative property, and in return treated each man in mercenary fashion.

World War I temporarily interrupted Wharton's fiction-writing career. She plunged into war work, organizing several refugee shelters, and took six orphans temporarily into her own home. She published a stream of articles urging America's involvement in the war. For her tireless work, she was made a Chevalier of the Legion of Honor by the French government in 1916.

Wharton published running memoirs of her war years in Paris, and later on, some forgettable works of fiction, rarely read today, that were as unsubtle as army recruitment posters. At the war's end, in 1918, she published *Summer*, which she privately nicknamed "hot Ethan," for its simmering sensuality and many parallels to Ethan Frome.

The Age of Innocence, considered by many to be Edith Wharton's finest novel, was published in 1920. The book is both a devastating critique and a nostalgic remembrance of a lost New York, set in the 1870s among the upper-crust society of Edith's parents' generation. Its hero, Newland Archer, is a young lawyer who has fallen in love with his conventional young fiancée's unconventional cousin, Ellen Olenska. Ellen is struggling to free herself from a brutal marriage to a decadent European aristocrat. The book deftly reveals the cruel hypocrisy of New York society and the unjust strictures forced on its women. Ellen's relatives ignore her husband's many sins, and try to force her back into marriage by cutting her off financially.

Newland, who has been enlisted by his wife's family to urge Ellen back to Europe, would like nothing more than to leave his young wife, May, and run away with Ellen himself. Ellen refuses this plan when she learns that Newland's wife is pregnant, and departs for Paris, having convinced her relatives that she will live alone.

The final chapter of the book jumps ahead in time twenty-six years. We see the wisdom of Newland's having sacrificed his passion for Ellen Olenska—which he still wistfully remembers as "the flower of life." Newland and May have had a stable and contented marriage, centered around the nurturing of their three children. The "age of innocence" of the title refers to Newland's previous naïveté—his belief that he and Ellen might have been able to enjoy an enduring love without the supports of a society whose code they would have violated had they eloped. Wharton shows that the traditional societal values that forced Newland to stay with his wife are clearly the root of much that is fine in American life, though society's unjust excesses are also amply demonstrated in the book.

Yet we also see that Newland's children will benefit from the erosion of this traditional morality. His son, for example, will marry a young woman who was born out of wedlock—a choice that would have been unthinkable in his father's day. With sadness the hero realizes that had he and Ellen been born thirty years later, the divorces they had contemplated would not have been scandalous, and would not have caused them to be banished from New York.

He ruminates on the society that has changed so rapidly in his lifetime, mentally comparing his daughter with his late wife:

Mary Chivers was as tall and fair as her mother, but large-waisted, flat-chested and slightly slouching, as the altered fashion required. Mary Chivers' mighty feats of athleticism could not have been performed with the twenty-inch waist that May Archer's azure sash so easily spanned. And the difference seemed symbolic; her mother's life had been as closely girt as her figure. Mary, who was no less conventional, and no more intelligent, yet led a larger life and held more tolerant views. There was good in the new order, too.

The public and the critical world alike embraced *The Age of Innocence*. Besides being beautifully and sensitively written, it linked the old and new worlds of a rapidly changing America. The book was awarded the Pulitzer Prize in 1921. Wharton was the first woman to win this coveted award, the purpose of which was to honor the American novel which "best present[s] the wholesome atmosphere of American life and the highest standard of American manners and manhood." Though pleased with the award, Wharton was appalled when she learned of the terms in which she'd been honored.

The 1920s and 1930s marked a decline in the quality of Edith Wharton's work, though her public recognition soared. In 1923 she was awarded an honorary doctor of letters degree by Yale University, which would not accept women students for another several decades. The American Academy of Arts and Letters, which also excluded women from membership, awarded her its gold medal in 1929.

The postwar world, with its materialism and sexual liberation, horrified Wharton. She abhorred the flappers of the 1920s, with their "painted faces," short skirts, and infantile manners. She saw around her a world of "raving chaos" of which her "feeble tales" could make but little sense. She had hoped that greater freedom for women would have resulted in their influencing the world at large with their nobler qualities. Instead she saw women as having been liberated into a meaningless promiscuity. Her books turned simplistic and preachy. Most important, Wharton appears to have lost touch with America, which had always been her best subject. The frivolous people she lampooned in books like *The Glimpses of the Moon* (1922) and *The Children* (1928) were sketchily modeled after the aimless hedonists who flocked to Europe in the twenties. They were a poor sampling of her countrymen, but the only Americans she had come into contact with for many years.

Despite failing health, Edith continued to work furiously during the last years of her life. She wrote her memoirs, *A Backward Glance*, in the early 1930s. In her old age, she supported many aged and infirm friends, relatives, and retired servants.

Wharton suffered a series of strokes in her last months of life. Her final summer was spent amid the gardens of her villa outside Paris. When she died on August 11, 1937 at the age of seventy-five, she was the most renowned American author, the grande dame of American letters.

Despite her many achievements, Wharton always considered hers to be a "half-talent." That her reputation has grown with the century sharply contradicts this opinion. In her lifetime, the younger generation of novelists who attacked an increasingly soulless, materialistic America admired her work greatly. The young Sinclair Lewis saw her as a mentor, and dedicated his 1922 novel *Babbitt* to her. She and the young F. Scott Fitzgerald were also admirers of each other's work.

The best of Wharton's books are as magnetic to readers today as they were when newly written. *Ethan Frome* has proved to be a perennial seller, its sales gaining momentum through the Depression and World War II as Americans identified with its bleak realism. In the 1970s, feminists began to herald *The House of Mirth*, *The Custom of the Country*, and *Summer* as important historical documents that captured the position of American women in perfect detail.

In her body of work, Edith Wharton broke ground for female writers generally. Books by women in Wharton's time and earlier had often been criticized for lacking the grandeur and scope of men's writing. The concerns of women's novels were largely limited to affairs of the heart and home, while men's books encompassed their broader experience of wars, the making and breaking of empires, wilderness adventure, and business. Wharton's books succeeded in linking the domestic sphere to society and the world at large.

There are seldom happy endings for the women in Wharton's novels who seek to break free from traditional roles; she wrote about the world as she saw it, not as she would have liked it to be. Despite her association in life with sophistication, wealth, and privilege, what remains most with the reader of Edith Wharton's work is her recognition of opportunities lost, and her sympathy for the thwarted life.

Chronology

▬▬▬▬▬▬

January 24, 1862	born in New York City
1866	leaves for six-year European trip with parents
1876	first poems published anonymously in *Atlantic Monthly* magazine
1878	*Verses*, first poetry collection, privately published
1885	marries Edward "Teddy" Wharton
1888	first meets Henry James
1891	first short story published in *Scribner's* magazine
1894–96	suffers a series of nervous breakdowns
1899	publishes first short-story collection, *The Greater Inclination*
1901	builds country home, The Mount, in Lenox, Massachusetts
1905	*The House of Mirth*, her fourth novel, becomes a best-seller and a critical success
1907	begins three-year affair with Morton Fullerton
1911	*Ethan Frome* published; The Mount sold
1913	divorces Teddy Wharton; settles permanently in Paris
1916	made a chevalier of the Legion of Honor by French government for war work
1921	awarded Pulitzer Prize for *The Age of Innocence*
1923	awarded honorary degree of doctor of letters by Yale University

1929	awarded gold medal by the American Academy of Arts and Letters
August 11, 1937	dies at Paris home

Further Reading

Wharton's Works

The Age of Innocence. New York: Macmillan 1986; originally published by D. Appleton, New York, 1920. Wharton's Pulitzer Prize–winning study of late nineteenth-century society and morals. This edition has an excellent introduction by Wharton biographer R. W. B. Lewis.

A Backward Glance. New York: D. Appleton–Century, 1934. Author's reminiscences and correspondence.

Ethan Frome. New York: Penguin, 1987; originally published 1911. Wharton's classic short novel, with an interpretive introduction by Wharton scholar Cynthia Griffin Wolff.

The House of Mirth. New York: Penguin, 1964; originally published by Scribner's, New York, 1905. Wharton's devastating critique of wasted womanhood, with an afterword by Louis Auchincloss.

Books About Wharton

Auchincloss, Louis. *Edith Wharton: A Woman in Her Time.* New York: Viking Press, 1971. Biography of the author with a special historical perspective, by one of her own class and pedigree.

Lewis, R. W. B. *Edith Wharton: A Biography.* New York: Harper & Row, 1975. The definitive biography of the author.

Willa Cather: Novelist of the Great Frontier

Long before she became one of the century's greatest and most original American authors, Cather was a successful journalist and editor who wrote a professional newspaper column while still an undergraduate at the University of Nebraska. Though in youth she fled the West, in middle age Willa Cather returned there again and again. She came to appreciate landscapes like the Mesa Verde in New Mexico, against which she is sketched here, as settings in which people could find their "essential selves."
(Library of Congress)

---

*B*orn in Virginia in 1873, Willa Cather at the age of nine moved with her family to the Nebraska frontier, where she lived what she later described as a "culturally deprived life" before escaping to college and a career as an East Coast journalist. But the lonely, hard life of the prairie made an imprint on her soul, and allowed her to identify with the immigrant neighbors she later depicted as heroes in *My Ántonia* and *O Pioneers!*—the great Nebraska novels she wrote in her middle age, in New York. Cather believed there were not enough American authors who wrote about the common people, and she tried to fill that gap herself. She was one of the first American authors to write of the immigrant pioneers who settled the West, and the first to highlight the role frontier women played in building the nation. Her best novels depict extraordinary, strong women.

Wilella Seibert Cather was born on December 7, 1873 in rural Back Creek, Virginia, the eldest of seven children born to Charles Cather, a sheep farmer who had studied law, and Mary Boak Cather. By the time she reached her teens, Cather had amended her first name to Willa in honor of two male relatives named William—an uncle who had been a Civil War hero, and her maternal grandfather, who had been a member of the Virginia legislature. But growing up, Cather was also heavily influenced by strong women—her mother, an imperious Southern belle, and her maternal grandmother, Rachel Boak. Cather was born in her grandmother's house, and it was she who taught Willa to read and write.

In the spring of 1883 Cather's family migrated to Webster County, Nebraska, following an uncle and her paternal grandparents. Although her relatives saw the move as one of opportunity—an escape from a depressed, post–Civil War South—to young Cather the long journey across country seemed to end in nowhere. She later wrote of her feelings on confronting the limitless prairie, where no mountains, trees, or houses stood: "I felt a good deal as if we had come to the end of everything—it was a kind of erasure of personality."

In the Nebraska of the late nineteenth century, Native Americans were losing much of their land. The United States government encouraged cultivation of the Great Plains through the Homestead Act of 1862, which allowed settlers to claim up to 160 acres if they farmed for six years. Easterners like the Cathers joined poor but hopeful European immigrants—Swedes, Germans, Norwegians, Danes, and Czechs—in the trek westward. Red Cloud, where Willa's father moved to open an insurance office after a year on the family farm, was by 1882 a boom town of 2,500.

From the start, Cather was fascinated by her Czech, Swedish, Norwegian, and German neighbors—her first contact with an older and grander culture which she would increasingly hunger for as she grew older. She loved visiting her European friends and listening to the stories they told of their native lands. Most of these neighbors were much less well off than the Cathers, and the hardships of the untamed prairie defeated many. The suicide of the father of Cather's friend and neighbor, a Czech girl named Annie Sadilek, later dramatized in *My Ántonia*, epitomized the despair that many immigrants felt at the bleakness of prairie life and their longing for the cultures they had left behind.

As a child, Cather was a tomboy, cutting her hair short and joining the boys in rough outdoor pursuits. She had good teachers at school, and was a bright, inquisitive child. She attended every traveling theatrical and musical production that passed through town, and eagerly sought out mentors. A German-Jewish couple introduced her to their native tongue; a local woman opened her ears to classical music; and an elderly neighbor taught her Greek and Latin. In her spare time Cather consumed Greek mythology and the works of Mark Twain, Robert Louis Stevenson, and Leo Tolstoy.

Cather's father borrowed money to send her to the University of Nebraska at Lincoln, where she quickly distinguished herself as a writer, though she had originally intended to study medicine. A professor was so impressed with her work that he passed along a paper she had written on the philosopher Thomas Carlyle to the *Nebraska State Journal*, Lincoln's daily newspaper, which published it. That professor, Will Owen Jones, was an editor at the paper, and quickly became another in Cather's long list of mentors. Soon, in addition to her many contributions to campus student publications, Cather was writing a regular theater column in the *Journal*. Cather's opinions, even at this early age, were strong and absolutely self-assured.

After graduating in 1895, Cather returned home to Red Cloud, but she soon left for Pittsburgh and a position as assistant editor at a new magazine for women, the *Home Monthly*. She chafed at the magazine's sickly-sweet tone and its vigilance in protecting its young female readers' "innocence." She herself often wrote stories in the action/adventure mode under male bylines, speaking in the first-person voice of a sailor or a cowboy. When the *Home Monthly* folded after a year, Cather found a position as an editor at the *Leader*, Pennsylvania's largest-circulation evening paper, and stayed there for three years.

In Pittsburgh, Cather traveled in theatrical circles, but steered clear of the bohemian lifestyle that she depicted in her early short story "Paul's Case." "Bohemia is pre-eminently the kingdom of failure," she wrote a friend in 1896. Instead, she pursued a strategy of hard work. During this time she met a number of artists and composers, and was especially drawn to the charismatic power of female opera stars. Throughout her literary career, her works would depict the contrasting backgrounds of her life—wild country and cultivated city, the barbaric and the genteel.

Seeking more time to write fiction, Cather left the *Leader* in 1900, and after working for two months as a translator in Washington, D.C., moved back to Pennsylvania, where she taught high school for five years, first in Pittsburgh, then in Allegheny. She moved into the family home of Isabelle McClung, a young woman she had met the year before and with whom she would cherish a strong and lifelong attachment. Late in life, Cather would confide to a friend that everything she wrote in her life, she wrote for Isabelle. In Pittsburgh, the two young women devoted themselves to art, and spent long evenings in Cather's attic room, where Willa wrote and Isabelle read. Cather finally made her long-awaited trip to Europe when the two traveled to Paris together in 1902. The trip was a cultural homecoming for

Cather. The landscape and architecture she had long known and loved from books and paintings moved her to produce a volume of rather mediocre, sentimental poetry, titled *April Twilights*, published the following year.

Meanwhile, Cather's stories, published in the *Home Monthly* and elsewhere, had caught the eye of the editor and publisher S. S. McClure, who ran both a publishing company and a magazine. She traveled to New York to meet McClure in 1903. While she was in his office, he called his staff in and soundly admonished them for rejecting the stories she had previously sent to the magazine. In 1905 the firm of McClure, Phillips published her first collection of stories, *The Troll Garden*. The following year Cather moved to New York to join the staff of *McClure's Magazine*, and by 1909 she had advanced to the post of managing editor.

The stories collected in *The Troll Garden* were mainly beginner pieces—autobiographical tales of talented midwesterners thwarted by a barren, closed-minded, culturally starved environment. In style, the stories emulated the drawing room elaborations of Henry James. Although the volume met with encouraging reviews, Cather quickly became ashamed of the book, recognizing its faults. The collection did yield one indisputable masterpiece, "Paul's Case," which is perhaps Cather's most anthologized story. Set in Pittsburgh, this story sets an effete young student—whose character was based on one of Cather's own pupils—against the suffocating Philistine background of the industrial city. Paul disdains authority and his bourgeois environment, and although no kind of artist himself, he is enraptured with drama and music, a perpetual hanger-on in theatrical circles. Expelled from high school for insubordination and barred from seeing his theatrical friends, Paul steals a large sum of money from the bank where his father has sent him to work. Posing as a wealthy young gentleman, Paul lives a life of reckless extravagance in New York City for a week before his discovery prefigures his suicide.

"Paul's Case" is a warning against the dangers of bohemian hedonism, told in a sort of lyrically tragic tone that recalls the

French writer Gustave Flaubert. Cather has an amazing ability to articulate the hero's point of view:

> When he reached the dining-room he sat down at a table near a window. The flowers, the white linen, the many-coloured wine glasses, the gay toilettes of the women, the low popping of corks, the undulating repetitions of the Blue Danube from the orchestra, all flooded Paul's dream with bewildering radiance. When the roseate tinge of his champagne was added—that cold, precious, bubbling stuff that creamed and foamed in his glass—Paul wondered that there were honest men in the world at all. This was what all the world was fighting for, he reflected; this was what all the struggle was about.

In 1908 Cather traveled to Europe again with Isabelle McClung, but on returning, set up house in Greenwich Village with another friend, Edith Lewis, a journalist who would be Cather's lifelong companion and biographer. Although the two women were close, it appears that Lewis quickly fell into a subservient role in her relationship with the strong-willed and demanding Cather.

On one of her assignments for *McClure's*, Cather met the writer Sarah Orne Jewett, a Maine native then living in Boston. Although the friendship between the two women writers was brief—Jewett died less than two years after their 1909 meeting—it was significant for Cather. Jewett encouraged the younger writer to use her rural Western upbringing as a literary subject: "One day you will write about your own country . . . One must know the world *so well* before one can know the parish." She also declared that Cather would have to set aside journalism if she ever hoped to truly improve as a fiction writer. "You must find your own quiet corner of life, and write from that to the world," she wrote in a letter.

In her writing, Cather was already beginning to reframe her view of her Western childhood. Cather's nostalgic short story "The Enchanted Bluff," published in *Harper's Weekly* in 1909, was a departure from her previous descriptions of the frontier as an oppressive, stifling place. This story laid bare the country's raw beauty:

> It was still dark, but the sky was blue with the last wonderful azure of the night . . . Day came suddenly, almost instantaneously. I turned for another look at the blue night, and it was gone. Everywhere the

birds began to call, and all manner of little insects began to chirp and hop about the willows. A breeze sprang up from the west and brought the heavy smell of ripened corn . . ."

In 1910, Cather set to work on her first novel, *Alexander's Bridge*, which was published in 1912 by Houghton Mifflin to strong reviews. Although Cather herself soon came to disdain the book, it was a well-fashioned work, showcasing a theme she would perfect in her later literary efforts—that of a lost or instinctive self that has been thwarted by modern life and materialistic pursuits.

Cather herself was dissatisfied with *Alexander's Bridge*, since it was written in a formal, literary style that she felt limited the ideas she was struggling to express. She immediately began work on a new novel, set in the Nebraska of her youth. In the spring of 1912, she left *McClure's* and took her first trip to the Southwest, whose wild, rugged landscape made a deep impression on her and would later figure strongly in such novels as *The Song of the Lark*, *Death Comes for the Archbishop*, and *The Professor's House*. She spent that summer in Red Cloud with her parents, where she did much of the on-location writing for her next novel, *O Pioneers!*, published in 1913.

O Pioneers!, which took its title from a Walt Whitman poem, is the book with which Willa Cather, at age forty, finally found her topic and voice. Written in a direct, natural, seemingly artless style, with a loose, episodic structure, *O Pioneers!* is the story of Alexandra Bergson, a Swedish-American pioneer woman who saves her family's struggling homestead after her father's death. Alexandra's devotion to the land, her struggles with her incompetent brothers, and her eventual prosperity are heroically depicted. "The history of every country begins in the heart of a man or woman," the opening narrative declares, ". . . the great fact was the land itself, which seemed to overwhelm the little beginnings of human society that struggled in its sombre wastes . . ."

Ever since her time at the *Home Monthly*, Cather had scorned "sentimental" women's writing that dealt with the emotional side of life, preferring the epic themes of the classics. In *O*

Pioneers! she created one of American literature's first true feminist heroines: the strong and brave Alexandra Bergson, whose greatest bond is with the land—"her mind was a white book, with clear writing about weather and beasts and growing things." There is a tragic romance in the novel—Alexandra's younger brother Emil's involvement with a married woman—which ends in death for the adulterous pair. Alexandra finds solace in marriage to a childhood friend, but the overarching theme of the book is the glory of one woman's conquest of the land.

With its blend of myth, realism, romance, and celebration of the rural American spirit, *O Pioneers!* was enthusiastically received by the critics and reading public alike. Cather's next novel, *The Song of the Lark*, published in 1915, was about a young Colorado-born opera singer's climb to fame and fortune. The novel drew from the life of her friend, the opera star Olive Fremsted, and in this book Cather reverted to the rather clunky, overly detailed Jamesian style of her earlier work. Cather was later critical of the book, recognizing a certain narrowness in its preoccupation with the frustrations of a young genius. Some years later, she cut the novel drastically. In 1914, while still working on *The Song of the Lark*, Cather traveled to Red Cloud for the summer. Visiting with her old friend and neighbor Annie Pavelka, formerly Annie Sadilek, she began to lay the groundwork for her next novel, *My Ántonia*.

In 1915, Cather again visited the Southwest and, accidentally stranded, spent a night on Mesa Verde in New Mexico with her friend Edith Lewis, a happenstance that made national news. Staying up all night and watching the sun rise from the natural rock formation, the one-time home of a vanished tribe of cliff-dwelling Native Americans, Cather was deeply affected by the beauty and mystical power she felt there. The experience would figure in a later novel, *The Professor's House*.

The year 1916 was a difficult one for Cather. Distraught over the marriage of her friend Isabelle McClung, she traveled to Taos, New Mexico, to Wyoming, and to Red Cloud, where she kept house for her ailing mother and received an honorary doctorate degree from her nearby alma mater, the University of Nebraska in Lincoln.

Returning to New York in the fall, Cather brought several completed chapters of *My Ántonia* with her, but was beginning to feel a new sense of sadness, almost of desolation. The world was changing. America was being drawn into the incomprehensible brutality of World War I, and faced with the impending deaths of her parents, Cather was coming to terms with her own mortality. A sense of bittersweet nostalgia for a lost time fired the writer to scour the past for meaning and hope. It was this mood that produced what many consider her most beautiful and heartfelt work.

In style, *My Ántonia*, published in 1918, follows the episodic, apparently plotless pattern of *O Pioneers!*, seeming to actually replicate the experience of memory itself. Through narrator Jim Burden, Cather's surrogate, who comes to Nebraska as a boy, the author relates anecdotally the experience of growing up on the prairie and the true stories of his immigrant neighbors. When Burden arrived there, Nebraska was "nothing but land: not a country at all, but the material out of which countries are made." The story of Ántonia, Jim's childhood friend, is related rather obliquely. Ántonia represents to Jim everything that is beautiful and memorable in a place also characterized by repression and hardship.

The book is neither a real romance nor a melodrama. Through Jim's almost unconcerned child's eye view, Cather simply tells the story of Ántonia Shimerda—her father's suicide, her work as a servant, her deception by a flashy railroad worker and consequent abandonment, and her life as a single mother. Yet neither Ántonia nor any of the struggling immigrants in the book are ever presented as victims; rather they are shown triumphing over circumstances through their endurance and faith. While the beleaguered Ántonia is finally seen in happy middle age, on a prospering farm with a husband and an adoring brood of children, Jim Burden, the supposedly "successful" one, has gone on to an unfulfilling city career and a childless and emotionally sterile marriage.

Ántonia is pictured as a sort of nature goddess, her identity one with the land: "She lent herself to immemorial human attitudes which we recognize by instinct as universal and true . . . She had only to stand in the orchard, to put her hand on a little crab tree and look up at the apples, to make you feel the goodness of planting and tending and harvesting at last."

Later, in an essay Cather wrote called "The Novel Demeuble," she said she sought to convey indirectly on the page a depth of emotion: "whatever is felt upon the page without being specifically named there . . . the emotional aura of the fact or the thing or the deed, that gives high quality to the novel or the drama." Throughout this novel, the author does precisely that, most often communicating through the landscape. When at twenty-one Jim returns from Harvard to his former home to see his old friend disgraced, living in isolation with her illegitimate baby, he is deeply moved.

> *I slept that night in the room I used to have when I was a little boy, with the summer wind blowing in at the windows, bringing the smell of the ripe fields. I lay awake and watched the moonlight shining over the barn and the stacks and the pond, and the wind-mill making its old dark shadow against the blue sky.*

At the book's close, Jim Burden, in a declaration to Ántonia, articulates all that the memory of her brave and inspiring childhood friends meant to Cather herself. "The idea of you is a part of my mind; you influence my likes and dislikes, all my tastes, hundreds of times when I don't realize it. You really are a part of me."

My Ántonia received good notices when it was published in 1918, solidifying Cather's reputation as an author. But she felt that its publisher, Houghton Mifflin, had done a lackluster job promoting the book, and in 1920 she signed on with Alfred A. Knopf. During this time, Cather was doing much of her writing in two East Coast wilderness havens she had recently discovered. Much of *My Ántonia* was written in mountainous Jaffrey,

New Hampshire, where Cather would eventually build a house and be buried. In 1921 she also began spending long stretches of time on isolated Grand Manan, a Canadian island off the coast of Maine.

In 1920, Cather published her next collection of stories, *Youth and the Bright Medusa*, which comprised the best stories from *The Troll Garden* and four new stories. Several of these stories again took up her favored theme of artists struggling for self-definition in a Philistine world. The collection was critically acclaimed, but even greater honors were to come.

In 1923, Cather was awarded the Pulitzer Prize for her World War I novel *One of Ours*, published the previous year. Cather had been deeply affected by the death of a young cousin of hers, and in this book she attempted to tell his story—that of a simple midwestern farmboy, hungering for cultural enrichment, who finds fulfillment in the cathedrals and art galleries of France before idealistically dying on the battlefield.

Although this book won her the Pulitzer—or perhaps because of it—the book was attacked by many critics. Coming out late, in 1923, into an atmosphere of postwar pessimism and disillusion expressed in literary works like T. S. Eliot's *The Waste Land*, Cather's novel appeared to whitewash the bloody debacle. Cather perhaps strayed too far from her own experience in writing about the war. Though she visited battlefields, she relied on secondary sources for her descriptions of battle scenes.

Writers like Ernest Hemingway, who had witnessed the war's senseless brutality firsthand and had written condemnatory tales of it, scorned Cather's depiction of romantic martyrdom. But ordinary readers—the many bereaved who hoped that their sons and brothers had died for a good cause—bought the book in droves.

One of Ours was highly critical of the materialism of modern American culture. This was a theme Cather would trumpet more strongly in subsequent works, as she contrasted the citified, money-centered life of "progress" with the merits of her pioneer childhood. Increasingly drawn to the past with its traditional spiritual values, she formally joined the Episcopal Church in 1922.

The early 1920s produced three strong Cather novels, each centered around aristocratic, worldly, cultivated people, each dissecting their flawed lives in a different way. Her 1923 short novel *A Lost Lady* was a profile of a female "gold digger" of the new West—an enigmatic work that presented its protagonist rather compassionately, withholding judgment. *My Mortal Enemy*, published in 1926, was a portrait of a destructive, manipulative woman, demonstrating Cather's abhorrence of a life lived strictly for personal gain.

By far the best novel of the three was *The Professor's House*, published in 1925. Its hero, Godfrey St. Peter, is a college professor who has achieved great worldly success but, like the hero of Cather's first novel, is spiritually estranged from the shallow society around him and from his grasping family.

In the later 1920s and beyond, when Cather was in her late fifties and sixties, her life became increasingly unhappy, despite her continuing literary success and fame. The deaths of her parents and old friends, anxiety over the need to live up to her reputation, depression, and bouts of illness led the writer to become obsessed with mortality. Happily for her readers, these sentiments found an outlet in perhaps her finest novel, *Death Comes for the Archbishop*, published in 1927.

Cather had by now revisited the Southwest several times, and had become fascinated with the era's colonial history, particularly the stories of the French missionaries sent by the Vatican to pacify warring, corrupt factions of the original Spanish missions. In her historical novel, her heroes, Bishop Jean Latour and Father Joseph Vaillant, are based on the real-life Jesuit missionaries Bishop Jean Baptiste Lamay and Father Joseph Machebeuf, French clerics who established a mission in Denver. Cather's ceaseless quest for meaning was reflected in her fascination with old, conservative structures—here the Catholic Church—as well as in her appreciation of Native American culture.

In her own life Willa Cather broke with traditions that had limited women's opportunities, yet in her writing she celebrated many values identified as conservative, such as the self-reliance of the American pioneers. In old age, she felt increasingly at odds with the materialism and soullessness she observed in post–World War I American society.
(Library of Congress)

Previous American writers—even up to F. Scott Fitzgerald, who was her junior—spoke of the American land as theirs by birthright, something to be conquered and plundered, ignoring the fact that the continent was already "settled" when Europeans arrived. But after visiting the ancient Indian dwellings at Mesa Verde, Cather felt she recognized the true ancestry of all Americans. In *Death Comes for the Archbishop*, a character observes the symbiosis between the Native Americans and their land:

> . . . *it was the Indian's way to pass through a country without disturbing anything; to pass and leave no trace, like a fish through the water, or birds through the air . . . The Hopi villages that were set upon rock mesas, were made to look like the rocks on which they sat, were imperceptible at a distance.*

This historical novel was the least autobiographical of Cather's works—a true departure—and was an immediate success.

In the fall of 1927, progress infringed upon Cather in a very concrete way: The Bank Street apartment building in Greenwich Village where she had lived with Edith Lewis for fifteen years was pulled down to make way for a new subway line. Cather spent much of the next two years traveling—to Red Cloud; to France, where her friend Isabelle McClung Hambourg was living with her husband; and to Quebec, which inspired her next work, *Shadows on the Rock*, published in 1931. The book was another historical study—this time of the French settlers in seventeenth-century French Canada—that stressed themes of pioneer ingenuity, family security, and maternal influence. Like its predecessor, it was a runaway success with readers, but many critics found it dull.

In 1929, Cather had been honored with an honorary doctorate from Yale University; in 1931 she was awarded two more honorary degrees—from Princeton and the University of California at Berkeley. The following year she published a fine collection of three long stories, each a backward-looking study in nostalgia, with the overall title *Obscure Destinies*. Each of the stories—"Old Mrs. Harris," which reflects memories of her grandmother; "Neighbor Rosicky," a loving portrait of a simple

Czech pioneer; and "Two Friends," about two men whose friendship is destroyed by the false rhetoric of politics—represents a reconciliation with the past. All three stories deal with themes of the dignity of rural labor and the spiritual vacuum human beings feel when they lose connection with the land. Here the elderly Rosicky recalls what led him, as an immigrant youth, to journey west from New York City:

> When the grass turned green in Park Place, and the lilac hedge at the back of Trinity Churchyard put out its blossoms, he was tormented by a longing to run away . . . The emptiness was intense, like the stillness in a great factory when the machinery stops and the belts and bands cease running. It was too great a change, it took all the strength out of one. Those blank buildings, without the stream of life pounding through them, were like empty jails.

In 1932, Cather settled into a Park Avenue apartment in New York City, also spending time in the two homes she had built in Jaffrey, New Hampshire and Grand Manan. As she entered old age Cather grew sterner, more judgmental about modern life and younger writers. The title of a book of reflective essays she published at this time, *Not Under Forty*, conveyed the separation of sensibility she felt from those who had grown up in the post–World War I "modern" world. As might be expected from such a strong admirer of the rugged individualist pioneer spirit, Cather was suspicious of the collectivist ethos of President Roosevelt's New Deal, along with psychoanalysis, Freudianism, Marxism, and social reform. Cather rejected the work of most of her modernist literary contemporaries, including the innovations of Gertrude Stein and the stark, self-examining plays of Eugene O'Neill. She adamantly refused all offers to have her books made into films.

Though she regarded the outside world coldly, Cather grew warmer and more generous to those she cherished from the past, often sending money to old friends such as Annie Pavelka in Red Cloud.

In 1935 Cather produced a dark novel, ironically titled *Lucy Gayheart*, about the doomed love affair of an aspiring midwestern musician. Honors continued to pour in throughout the

1930s and 1940s—the Howell Medal for Fiction, the Prix Femina Americaine from France, the Gold Medal from the National Institute of Arts and Letters, as well as another honorary degree, this time from Smith College.

As she saw the end of her life nearing, Cather warned her friends not to share her letters with the press, and burned as many of them as she could find. Always a perfectionist, she destroyed many "unworthy" manuscripts, fearing they would come to publication after her death. She was troubled by illness—appendicitis attacks that would culminate in an operation in 1942, and wrist trouble that curtailed her writing. In 1938, two deaths—that of Isabelle McClung Hambourg, and of her favorite brother, Douglas—came as debilitating blows.

The onset of World War II cast a further shadow on Cather's twilight years, and she looked further and further into the past for consolation and meaning. Her last completed novel, *Sapphira and the Slave Girl*, published in 1939, examined the problematic relations among members of a slave-holding southern family, and marked the only time she drew from her southern background.

Cather published few works in her last years. Her final manuscript, somehow saved from complete annihilation, was about two young men of medieval France on a spiritual quest. Tentatively titled "Hard Punishments," it showed Cather journeying even further into the past and its traditional religious values.

Cather died of a cerebral hemorrhage on April 24, 1947 in New York City, where, in ill health for several months, she had been nursed by Edith Lewis. She was buried in Jaffrey, New Hampshire. On her gravestone, she quoted a slice of her own prose, from *My Ántonia*:

> At any rate: that is happiness; to be dissolved into something complete and great.

Willa Cather is revered and remembered as a writer of the first rank, and as a celebrator of a vanished pioneer ethic.

Though during her own lifetime her fame rested largely on her Nebraska novels, her more urbane works, like *The Professor's House* and *Death Comes for the Archbishop*, have also stood the test of time. Her literary reputation has grown steadily through this century, as feminists and other scholars dissect and hail her early portraits of strong, independent women.

Cather's work stands oddly apart from that of other modernist writers, with their self-conscious, sometimes ostentatious innovations in style, à la Gertrude Stein. She is often viewed as a literary descendant of the British novelist Thomas Hardy, who also wrote lovingly of rural working peoples' bond with the land.

In Cather's novel *The Song of the Lark*, the young heroine, Thea Kronberg, coming across pottery that was fashioned by Native American women, realizes that all art is "an effort to make a sheath, a mould in which to imprison for a moment the shining elusive element which is life itself." The statement serves as an articulation of Cather's own creative philosophy. In a newspaper interview she once said that she wanted her readers to think of her work as "not stories at all, but life itself." The fifteen books of fiction Cather left behind testify to her success in achieving this aim.

Chronology

―――

December 7, 1873	born in Back Creek, Virginia
1883	migrates to Nebraska with family
1895	graduates from University of Nebraska
1896	moves to Pittsburgh to take position at *Home Monthly*
1903	publishes poetry collection, *April Twilights*
1905	first story collection, *The Troll Garden*, published by McClure, Phillips
1906	joins staff of *McClure's Magazine* as managing editor in New York
1912	publishes first novel, *Alexander's Bridge*
1913	publishes *O Pioneers!*
1918	publishes *My Ántonia*
1923	wins Pulitzer Prize for *One of Ours*
1927	publishes *Death Comes for the Archbishop*
1929	elected to membership in the National Institute of Arts and Letters; receives honorary doctorate from Yale University
1930	receives Howells Medal for Fiction from the American Academy of the National Institute of Arts and Letters for *Death Comes for the Archbishop*
1931	receives honorary doctorates from the University of California at Berkeley and Princeton University; *Shadows on the Rock* published
1932	*Obscure Destinies* published

1933	awarded Prix Femina Americaine for *Shadows on the Rock*; receives honorary degree from Smith College
1938	elected to membership in the Academy of the National Institute of Arts and Letters
1940	*Sapphira and the Slave Girl* published
1944	awarded National Institute of Arts and Letters Gold Medal
April 24, 1947	dies in New York City

Further Reading

Cather's Works

Death Comes for the Archbishop. New York: Alfred A. Knopf, 1927, 1988. A new edition of one of the author's finest works.

My Ántonia. Boston: Houghton Mifflin, 1918, 1988. The beloved novel, augmented by Cather scholar Doris Grumbach's insightful foreword.

Willa Cather: Early Novels and Short Stories. New York: Literary Classics of the United States, 1987. This wide-ranging omnibus includes Cather's first story collection, *The Troll Garden*, as well as *O Pioneers!*, *The Song of the Lark*, *My Ántonia*, and *One of Ours*.

Books About Cather

Bonham, Barbara. *Willa Cather*. Philadelphia: Chilton, 1970. Comprehensive and reader-friendly biography.

Lewis, Edith. *Willa Cather Living*. 1953. Reprint. New York: Octagon Books, 1976. Memoirs of the author and her writing life, by her longtime companion, the journalist Edith Lewis.

Gertrude Stein
The Great Innovator

*Gertrude Stein's Roman profile and mannish looks
were trademarks, along with her irreverent wit and
easygoing attitude. Her reputation as an influential
and eccentric personality at
the center of a Paris-based circle of modernist artists
and writers preceded her own literary success.*
(Library of Congress)

*A*t the same time that Edith Wharton and Willa Cather were
producing their stories and novels in the style of meticulous
realism, across the Atlantic Ocean another American woman
writer was making a name for herself with fanciful literary

experiments that bore little resemblance to the real world, and even less to works of fiction that had come before.

Gertrude Stein was famous for ignoring convention in her writing and in every other aspect of her life. She drew her inspiration not from history, mythology, or the great masters of prose, but from the bizarre abstract canvases of the exploding modern art scene.

"I am the most important writer writing today," Stein wrote confidently in her 1938 autobiography. Few of her contemporaries would have agreed that she was her era's most important writer, but nearly all of them had to admit that she was an extraordinary personality. The power of her approval or disapproval was unrivaled in Paris's artistic and literary world in the first several decades of this century. Among American authors we consider great, Stein is an unusual case, since it is her influence over other writers, such as Ernest Hemingway, more than her body of work itself, that is historically significant in modern literature. She is legendary for her quips, her humorously egotistical and irreverent personality, and the role her Paris salon played in the development of a generation of pioneering painters and writers.

Gertrude Stein was born in 1874 in Allegheny, Pennsylvania, the fifth child and second daughter of Daniel Stein and the former Amelia Keyser, both German-Jewish immigrants. Her father had only a third-grade education, but, raised in a prosperous merchant family, had built up a successful furniture business. The Stein family moved to Vienna, Austria in 1875, when Gertrude was still a baby, following new business interests of her father. There the Steins lived the comfortable life of the Victorian middle class, with a Hungarian governess and a Czech tutor attending the children.

That Gertrude was the youngest child, and constantly doted on, set the mold for her adult personality. When she was a toddler, her aunt wrote of her to her father, who was living temporarily in Paris, "Our little Gertie is a little Schnatterer [chatterer]. She talks all day long and so plainly. *She outdoes them all.*"

Gertrude's first words were uttered in German, and the fact that English was a second language to both of her parents had no small effect on her later writing, leading to a fascination with simple words and their many different meanings.

Stein had a happy childhood. When she wrote her autobiography in 1938, she commented on being the youngest: "You are privileged, nobody can do anything but take care of you, that is the way I was and that is the way I still am."

In 1879, the Steins lived for a time near Passy, France, where Gertrude attended boarding school. In 1880, her father moved the family to Oakland, California, near San Francisco, where he had obtained a position as an executive in a trolley company. The Steins rented a large house on the edge of Oakland, where they enjoyed what she later described as "half-city, half-country" living. Stein's life in America began in this relatively free-thinking, ethnically and racially diverse environment. Neighbors included the young Isadora Duncan and her large bohemian family. Isadora would play a major role in developing modern dance in the early decades of the twentieth century.

Stein attended a coeducational public school, but spent most of her free time with her brother Leo, two years her senior, who was always her greatest friend. With him she hiked, swam, and rambled over the countryside, sometimes pitching in to help a farmer neighbor at harvest time. The two siblings avidly read the works of Mark Twain, Jules Verne, and Shakespeare, and devoured texts on history and science.

At school Gertrude was clever and precocious, but not conscientious, showing early evidence of her lifelong indifference to rules. When Gertrude was fourteen, her mother died of cancer. Her father was a tyrant, and to him Stein credited her lifelong aversion to all authorities and father figures. Her antiauthoritarian suspicions were aroused by the rise of fascism in Europe in the 1930s, when she wrote that "there was too much fathering going on."

Daniel Stein died in 1891, and as Gertrude later irreverently wrote, "Our life without a father began a very pleasant one." Leo and Gertrude moved to San Francisco to live with their oldest brother, twenty-six-year-old Michael, who also worked for the trolley company. Michael would become so successful that he was able to support his younger siblings for the rest of their lives.

In 1892, after Leo began studies at Harvard, Gertrude went to live with her maternal relatives in Baltimore. She enjoyed the lively seaport city and reveled in its southern flavor, but the next year she followed her brother to Cambridge, Massachusetts, where she attended classes at Harvard's new women's division, then called Harvard Annex (renamed Radcliffe College in 1894). Having completed only a few years of high school in Oakland, and lacking the Latin required for entrance, Stein did not at first intend to pursue a bachelor's degree. She showed such promise, however, that the entrance requirements were waived, and soon she became a star student of psychology. She found a mentor in the pioneer psychoanalyst William James, brother of the writer Henry James and one of the greatest philosophers of his day.

At Harvard, Stein pursued her independent ways. One beautiful spring day, a day on which she was scheduled to take an exam, she showed up only to write at the top of her paper, "I am so sorry but really I do not feel a bit like an examination today." James sent her this reply: "Dear Miss Stein, I understand perfectly how you feel. I often feel like that myself," and gave her the highest marks in his course!

James conducted experiments in "automatic" or "stream of consciousness" writing, in which subjects wrote down their unedited, free-associative thoughts. Much of the writing Stein would later produce has the appearance of being written in this completely free way, released from her mind unedited, without following traditional literary formats.

Such endeavors were some years in the future; her primary focus at Harvard remained science, and in 1896, while she was still an undergraduate, the results of experiments she conducted in human motor automation under James were published in the *Psychological Review*.

Stein's intellectual curiosity and assertive but easygoing personality made her a favorite among her professors. Though she was short, stout, and unstylish, eschewing all attempts to make herself more attractive, she had few social worries, since she was always included in her brother Leo's active social life.

In 1897 she failed the Latin examination, and was consequently denied her bachelor's degree. However, so strong were her recommendations from William James and her other professors that she was admitted to Johns Hopkins Medical School in Baltimore, where Leo was also studying. (She was awarded her B.A. from Radcliffe the following spring.)

In Baltimore, Stein set up a household with her brother under the supervision of a housekeeper, who became the model for the title character in a later story, "The Good Anna." Leo, full of passion for the developing arts and sciences he'd observed during a recent trip around the world, began holding salons—weekly social events with a progressive intellectual focus.

In medical school Stein did well at first, but after Leo left to study art and poetry in Florence in 1900, her interest flagged. She found that there was too much emphasis on abnormality and disease in her courses, and later wrote that "the normal is so much more simply complicated and interesting."

In 1901 Stein failed her final exams and dropped out of medical school, but her years in Baltimore were not wasted. As a medical student, she had gained a broad exposure to humanity, venturing into African-American and immigrant slum neighborhoods to deliver babies and tend the sick. Before the decade was out she would document her experiences in a book called *Three Lives*, published in 1909.

In 1902, Stein moved to London with Leo, and began to seriously pursue a literary career. She spent hours reading literature and history in the British Museum, and began to write fiction. She drafted two works the following year while briefly living in New York—the short story "Fenhurst," loosely based on a lesbian scandal at Bryn Mawr College, and a novel, published much later under the title *Things As They Are*, that reflected questions of sexuality that had been troubling Stein during her last few years at medical school.

This book also marked the start of her interest in examining personality types—a constant theme in her work. In 1902 Stein also began drafting *The Making of Americans*. In this work, she began to explore the phenomenon of repetition in history and in individuals' lives. She felt that repetition was the reality of human experience, that events and personality types replicate themselves ad infinitum, with only minor changes.

In 1903, Stein settled with her brother Leo in Paris at 27 rue de Fleurus, on the Left Bank. Leo, who was studying painting, began to collect modern art, which most galleries still refused to exhibit. Leo began to befriend artists like Henri Matisse, Paul Cézanne, and Pablo Picasso, and they soon became regular visitors to the Steins' flat. Soon it became fashionable for Americans visiting Paris to stop in at the Steins' to view the pictures and sometimes meet the artists themselves. To control the growing stream of guests, the Steins formalized the visits into weekly "salons."

Gertrude and Leo became notorious revelers about town. They both smoked cigars and wore corduroy suits and sandals and laughed so loudly that they were evicted from the Café Royal. For Stein French life offered "independence from American thinking." With regard to writing, she enjoyed being "alone with her English," and found that her second country was the perfect vantage point from which to write about her first.

In 1905 she began writing *Three Lives*, a collection of three long stories profiling three working-class American women. "The Good Anna" and "The Gentle Lena" followed the lives of two German immigrant servants; "Melanctha" charted the progress of a passionate young African-American woman. Stein approached her analysis of each woman not in terms of her being representative of a caste or ethnic group, but, reflective of her psychological training, of a personality type—the hard-working, self-sacrificing Anna, the passive Lena, and the complicated Melanctha.

What is most remarkable about these stories is their true-to-life speech, which delivers to the reader language as it is actually spoken, completely stripped of the unnatural formality common to most nineteenth-century fiction.

In their cubist paintings, Cézanne and Picasso would combine different aspects of an object in the same work to analyze its form and mass. Stein used the same technique with language; by repeating a statement with slight alterations, she tried to show the different meanings of common words, with heightened impact. Here a varied repetition renders the many shades of emotion experienced by Melanctha's lover, Jeff Campbell:

> *Jeff never, even now, knew what it was that moved him. He never, even now, was ever sure, he really knew what Melanctha was, when she was herself, and honest. He thought he knew, and then there came to him some moment, just like one, she really woke him up to be strong in him. Then he really knew he could know nothing. He knew then, he never could know what it was she really wanted with him. He knew then, he never could know what it was he felt inside him. It was all so mixed up inside him.*

"Melanctha," perhaps Stein's finest piece of fiction, is the haunting story of the life and death of a young woman on a doomed quest for love, sexual passion, and an understanding of the world. She is thwarted in her quest by her own restless nature: "Melanctha Herbert was always losing what she had in wanting all the things she saw. Melanctha was always being left when she was not leaving others . . . She was always full with mystery and subtle movements and denials and vague distrusts and complicated disillusions." She is contrasted with her lover, Jeff Campbell, a young doctor, who represents a temperate and conservative personality type.

Although *Three Lives* is the one work of Stein's on whose quality critics today agree, at the time of its completion in 1906 it was shunned by no fewer than three commercial publishers. Stein finally paid to have it privately printed in 1909.

She sent her first work in print to friends, famous writers, and critics. The British writer H. G. Wells responded enthusiastically, but even Stein's mentor, William James, confessed that he had begun it and put it away. Stein was unfazed by the public's early indifference, and remained steadfast in her belief in herself. In 1906 she sat for a portrait by Picasso, and she saw a clear affinity between her work and his. She stuck by the modern painters through their unpopular cubist phase, when even her brother Leo had stopped buying their works.

In 1907, Stein's sister-in-law brought with her on a visit to Paris another woman from San Francisco, Alice Toklas. By 1908 Toklas was typing up the gargantuan manuscript of *The Making of Americans*, and the following year she moved into the Steins' flat. Toklas was both Gertrude's handmaiden—selflessly catering to Stein's secretarial and personal needs—and her lover. Buoyed by the unwavering worship of her new acolyte as well as by the publication of her book, Gertrude now began to dominate the Saturday evening soirees.

In 1911 Stein completed *The Making of Americans*, and began the long and arduous task of finding a publisher. Between 1910 and 1912 she wrote *Tender Buttons*, a book of "prose still lifes" in which, she later explained, she tried to express the rhythm of the visible world. By now Stein was celebrated enough, through visitors' tales of her life in Paris, to attract the interest of the literary world, and in 1914, Donald Evens, a New York publisher, bought *Tender Buttons*.

In this work Stein followed in the footsteps of nineteenth-century symbolist writers who had aimed to portray sensory perceptions in revolutionary ways, leading to a type of writing in which words are detached from their meanings. The writer's message is relayed through suggestions, rather than through a logical relating of facts. While *Tender Buttons* brought Stein attention and boosted her fame as an iconoclast, it was roundly derided, and in America it inspired a stream of parodies.

Much of Stein's writing during this period demanded a great deal from her readers, and reflected her often self-indulgent personality. In her autobiography she would write,

"It takes a lot of time to be a genius, you have to sit around so much doing nothing really doing nothing." She slept late each day and never hurried, and the ponderous rhythm of her life was reflected in her prose. She never edited or rewrote, but kept repeating with variations, writing alone late into the night, often until dawn.

Stein was in London trying to solicit the interest of a British publisher when World War I broke out, but she quickly rushed back to Paris. At the same time, Leo returned to America with his share of the art collection, and Gertrude and Toklas took over the rue de Fleurus flat.

By 1915, with World War I in full swing, Paris was void of artists and transatlantic visitors. Bored, Stein and Toklas traveled to Palma de Mallorca to see the running of the bulls—a spectacle she later recommended to Ernest Hemingway, who put it to legendary literary use. Stein and Toklas volunteered in the war effort, using her Ford to transport supplies to the French wounded. Stein enjoyed the company of American soldiers, and questioned them relentlessly about the minor details of their lives. The French government later awarded Stein and Toklas the Medaille de la Reconnaissance Française for their activities during the war.

When Stein returned to Paris in 1919, she found it a changed city. The circle of artists over which she had presided had broken up. In the artists' place, and soon to fill Gertrude's salon, were the embittered young American men, too disillusioned by the war to go home, whom Stein named "the lost generation." Among this group were Ernest Hemingway and F. Scott Fitzgerald, and they would dominate the social and literary life of Paris through the 1920s.

This new generation of young writers not only took Stein's work seriously, but were inspired by it. Sherwood Anderson was among those inspired. His critically acclaimed first novel, *Winesburg, Ohio* (1919), a study in stark realism, owes a debt to "Melanctha." In 1921, Anderson journeyed to Paris and presented himself to Stein, and the two became close and lifelong friends.

Stein was at the center of Parisian cultural and social life during the heady decade of the 1920s. Young writers who quaked at meeting the influential writer and hostess were surprised to find her open and amiable in person. These young writers were attracted to Stein's proclamations, such as her assertion that "the past did not matter." Just as modern artists had earlier stopped trying to duplicate real life on canvas, so Stein sought to break the chains that traditional narration imposed on writers. Her constant returns to a point of beginning—writing in a continuous present tense—went against the Victorian narrative concept of beginning, middle, and end.

In 1922, Sherwood Anderson sent a young American journalist whose fiction was then unpublished to meet Stein. Twenty-three-year-old Ernest Hemingway gave Stein his unpublished stories for criticism, and her influence on his work is clear—particularly in his use of short, declarative sentences, his abandonment of the comma, and his use of simple language and of repetition.

Stein gave the fledgling writer great encouragement, and in 1923 Stein and Toklas stood as godmothers to the Hemingways' first child. But this closeness was short-lived; after Hemingway published a vicious parody of Sherwood Anderson's work in 1926, Stein cut off all relations with the young writer, finding his action unforgivable. Still Hemingway remembered her in his own memoir of Paris in the twenties, *A Moveable Feast*: "She had such a personality that when she wished to win anyone over to her side she could not be resisted."

Before their break, Hemingway gave a boost to his mentor's career while he was working as assistant editor at the important literary magazine *The Transatlantic Review*. He persuaded its editor, the English writer Ford Madox Ford, to begin publishing her opus *The Making of Americans* in serialized form. Only a few installments of the work appeared before the magazine folded, but it was sanction enough to arouse the interest of a New York publisher, Robert McAlmon, whose Contact Editions brought out the volume in 1925.

In 1926 Stein lectured at Oxford and Cambridge universities in England. The English writer Harold Acton, then an undergraduate at Oxford, wrote that her incomprehensible lecture was "the litany of an Aztec priestess . . . uttered in a friendly American voice . . . What a contrast between manner and matter!" Among her unique perspectives was that "clarity is of no importance because no one listens," and that she had learned about punctuation from listening to her French poodle lap from its water dish. Meanwhile, American poet Marianne Moore and the writer Katherine Anne Porter were giving positive reviews to *The Making of Americans* back in Stein's native land.

In the late 1920s, Stein began to collaborate with the American composer Virgil Thomson, who was fascinated with her work, finding music in its rhythms. Their subject was "Lives of the Saints," which was later produced as a theatrical piece titled *Four Saints in Three Acts*. Stein was fascinated with saints as extreme beings who were set apart, like geniuses—among whose ranks she counted herself. True to her current form, the work was short on plot, consisting of a series of fragmented scenes.

In 1931 the American critic Edmund Wilson included Stein in *Axel's Castle*, his critical analysis of modernist writers. Although his reviews of Stein were mixed, he approached her work without derision or parody. Stein deemed it a tremendous and, of course, well-deserved honor to be scrutinized along with only five other important writers—including T. S. Eliot and James Joyce—whom Wilson considered key innovators.

For years, Stein's friends had been prompting her to write her memoirs. She was uninterested in this kind of writing, but agreed to the project if Toklas would write it. Toklas postponed the endeavor indefinitely, and finally in 1932 Stein produced *The Autobiography of Alice B. Toklas*. The book was actually a biography of Stein, as if written by her friend—the actual author's identity was given away only on the final page. The book, quickly bought by publishers Harcourt, Brace in New York, was witty, funny, clear, and readable, and for this reason sold briskly—the first of Stein's books to do so.

In Toklas's voice, Stein had a platform from which to blow her own horn: "[Stein] realizes that in English literature she is the only one. She has always known it and now she says it." She gave herself credit for virtually discovering modern art, and for "creating" Ernest Hemingway. Readers and critics hailed the emergence of "the real Miss Stein," and were puzzled: If she was capable of writing in this highly entertaining, comprehensible fashion, why didn't she do it all the time?

America fell in love with the picture of Stein presented in *The Autobiography*—a loveable eccentric, walking the streets of Paris with her giant white poodle, or recklessly driving in her enormous black Ford. This brilliant method of self-publicity finally brought Stein, at sixty, the glory she had always craved. But critics hoping for "the new Stein" would be disappointed with her next work. *Four in America* was a ponderous and esoteric study of Henry James, George Washington, Ulysses S. Grant, and Wilbur Wright.

In 1934 Stein traveled to her native country for the first time in thirty years for the Broadway premiere of *Four Saints in Three Acts*, which featured an all-black cast. She was taken aback to find the news of her arrival flashing in neon lights across a building in Times Square, but was soon comforted by the atmosphere of lionization that enveloped her.

While in America, she embarked on a college lecture tour. An Amherst student who attended her lecture commented, "I was dead against her and I just went to see what she looked like and then she took the door of my mind right off its hinges and now it's wide open." When questioned on philosophy she said, "I do not even know whether there is a question, let alone having an answer for a question."

In Chicago she befriended Thornton Wilder, who claimed her as his greatest literary influence. His play *Our Town*, in its aim to recreate the conscious experience of an ordinary day in life, is clearly influenced by Stein's work.

In 1937, Stein's literary output was temporarily disrupted when she lost the lease on the rue de Fleurus flat, her home for more than thirty years. She soon found a congenial new home nearby, and in 1938 resumed work, producing *Everybody's Autobiography*, her own life story under her own byline. Like the earlier autobiography, it was entertaining reading filled with her trademark egotism.

In 1939 she wrote *Paris France*, a tribute to her adopted country. The following year, when World War II began in earnest, Stein and Toklas were forced to stay in Bilignin, in the south of France, where they had leased a house and spent the summer months since 1931. From there, Stein sent dispatches from the war to the *Atlantic Monthly* in America. A novel she wrote during the war years, *Mrs. Reynolds*, used an animal allegory to convey the experience of living in occupied territory under the threat of Hitler.

In 1939, all Americans had been warned to leave France immediately, but Stein and Toklas decided to stay. At seventy, Stein threw herself into the rigors of village life in wartime, finding substitutes for soap, gasoline, and firewood. While waiting out the war in Bilignin, Stein wrote one of her finest books. *Wars I Have Seen*, published in 1945, was not only a journal of her life during the current war, but an examination of how her youth had been affected by the Civil and Boer wars.

In 1943 Stein and Toklas, having lost the lease on their house in Bilignin, moved to nearby Culoz. Again the two elderly women were advised by the consulate to leave. They were both enemy aliens and Jews in a Nazi-occupied country, and therefore were in grave danger. Stein was childishly unheeding of this peril, and perhaps her lifelong complacent certainty that she would be taken care of worked as some sort of magical protection—the two old women were saved due to the beneficence of the mayor of Culoz, who kept their names off all official records.

After D Day, Stein was again in the spotlight, broadcasting to American troops in Europe. She returned to Paris in 1944, and found her flat and its priceless collection of modernist paintings miraculously intact. She celebrated in the company of the thousands of American GIs who flooded Paris. In old age, she had found another fascinating milieu over which to preside. *Brewsie and Willie*, published in 1945, was a tribute to her young soldier friends. At seventy-one, Stein was at the height of her literary powers, the ordeal and triumph of the war prompting her to voice clear and original opinions on social issues and world events. She toured U.S. army bases in Germany, Austria, and Belgium and published articles in *Life* magazine and *The New York Times* about the GIs in Europe.

Stein's last year was an active one. Despite an attack of stomach pain November 1945, she kept forging ahead with creative projects, again working with the composer Virgil Thomson, this time on an opera based on the life of the suffragist Susan B. Anthony.

On July 19, 1946, she had another attack of stomach pain while en route to her country home, and was rushed to the American Hospital at Neuilly. The diagnosis was cancer. The doctors advised against operating, but Stein insisted, and the surgery was set for July 27. In the days before the surgery, her room was flooded with flowers and telegrams from friends, fans, and well-wishers. Before going under the anesthetic, she paraphrased herself by asking Toklas, "What is the answer?" Toklas was silent. Stein continued, "In that case, what was the question?" Stein died after the operation without regaining consciousness.

───────

Gertrude Stein is remembered as the difficult and idiosyncratic author of two or three outstanding works and a dozen or so original but impenetrable others. She achieved mixed results, at best, in her attempt to do with words what modern artists had done with painting. Stein's most enduring legacy is as cultural guru to a new generation of writers—as a theorist of language and literature whose prose innovations were stepping-stones for Ernest Hemingway and others seeking revolutionary new means of expression.

Stein's short, bald declarative sentences, critic Edmund Wilson said, made the complicated grammar of the nineteenth century seem obsolete. And "behind her limpid and slightly monotonous sentences," the critic wrote, "one becomes aware of her masterly grasp of the organisms, contradictory and indissoluble, which human personalities are."

One thing most critics agree on today is that Gertrude Stein changed the face of literature. She had once vowed that in her writing she wanted to kill off the nineteenth century. Unquestionably, she achieved her goal.

Chronology

▬▬▬▬▬

February 3, 1874	born in Allegheny, Pennsylvania
1875	moves with family to Vienna, Austria
1880	moves with family to Oakland, California
1892	moves to Baltimore after deaths of both parents
1893	enters Harvard Annex
1896	publishes "Normal Motor Automatism" in *Psychological Review*
1897	enters Johns Hopkins School of Medicine in Baltimore
1901–2	drops out of medical school; joins brother Leo in London
1903	drafts *The Making of Americans* and *Things As They Are* in New York; settles with Leo at 27 rue de Fleurus, Paris
1904	begins purchasing Paul Cézanne's art
1905	meets Pablo Picasso; begins *Three Lives*
1907	meets Alice Toklas
1909	*Three Lives* published
1914–18	*Tender Buttons* published; does war work in Alsace and Perpignan
1921	meets Sherwood Anderson
1922	meets Ernest Hemingway; awarded the Medaille de la Reconnaissance Française for war work
1924	*The Making of Americans* serialized in *The Transatlantic Review*
1932	completes *The Autobiography of Alice B. Toklas*

1934–35	*Four Saints in Three Acts* premieres on Broadway; makes lecture tour of the United States
1943	moves with Toklas to south of France
1944	returns to Paris; broadcasts to American troops
1945	tours American bases in occupied Germany
July 27, 1946	dies in France following cancer operation

Further Reading

Stein's Works

The Autobiography of Alice B. Toklas, 1933. Reprint. New York: Cooper Square Publishers, 1971. Stein's memoirs under the byline of her friend. Full of wit and humorous anecdotes about the expatriate artist community in Paris.

Three Lives. New York: Grafton, 1909. These compelling psychological portraits are the best and most accessible fiction Stein produced.

Wars I Have Seen. New York: Random House, 1945. Stein is at her best in these memoirs of World War II and before.

Books About Stein

Benstock, Shari. *Women of the Left Bank: Paris 1900–1940*. Austin: University of Texas Press, 1986. Women writers and issues of feminism in the expatriate Paris community. Djuna Barnes, Jean Rhys, and others profiled, in addition to Stein and Toklas.

Hobhouse, Janet. *Everybody Who Was Anybody: A Biography of Gertrude Stein*. New York: G.P. Putnam's Sons, 1975. An entertaining biography that discusses the writer's works within the context of her influences.

Mellow, James R. *Charmed Circle: Gertrude Stein & Company*. New York: Praeger, 1974. The phenomenon of Stein's Paris salon and how it shaped a generation of artists and writers.

Katherine Anne Porter "It All Happened"

Katherine Anne Porter led an adventurous life that began with an impoverished, neglected childhood and included four failed marriages and relationships with Communist revolutionaries and high-ranking Nazi officials. Her fiction scrutinizes the complexities of human nature and attempts to trace the roots of the evil she saw as so prevalent in this century.
(Library of Congress)

*D*enver, Colorado, October, 1918. The streets are filled with hearses carrying casualties of a mysterious influenza virus that has swept the nation, killing thousands. A war is raging in Europe, adding to the sense of dread.

A young woman reporter, far away from friends and family, is nearly broke and living in a shabby rooming house when the flu virus strikes. When she becomes ill, her landlady wants to put her out on the street, but a fellow lodger, a young soldier about to leave for the battlefront of World War I, prevents this. He nurses the young woman and arranges to have her taken to a hospital. There she is left behind screens to die, surrounded by the corpses of those already claimed by the plague. She lies unconscious with a 105 degree fever for nine days. Then a group of interns experimenting with lost-cause cases tries injecting her with strychnine. The poison finally defeats the virus, and the young woman awakes to find herself and her world dramatically altered. For while she lay unconscious, she experienced a glorious glimpse of the afterlife, and now finds her body "a curious monster," the world around her a colorless, dull place. She learns that two earthshaking things have oc- curred during her illness: the war has ended, and the young soldier who had nursed her, and with whom she had quickly fallen in love, had been infected with the virus and died.

The young woman in this story is both the heroine of Kath- erine Anne Porter's short novel, *Pale Horse, Pale Rider*, and Katherine Anne Porter herself. The situation and the young soldier are both drawn from real life, and in real life the young newspaper reporter emerged from her brush with death deeply affected, holding a new clarity of vision and a mission—a determination to write fiction, she declared in a letter to her sister soon after her recovery, "as well as anyone in America."

Katherine Anne Porter achieved her goal in a career that spanned six decades of a tumultuous century.

Callie Russel Porter was born on May 15, 1890 in a log cabin in Indian Creek, Texas, the second daughter and fourth child of Harrison Boone Porter—an indirect descendant of pioneer Daniel Boone—and Mary Alice Jones Porter.

Porter described herself as "the grandchild of a lost war": Her father's family had been prosperous farmers recently moved to

Texas from Kentucky before the Civil War, but had struggled to eke out a living after the war. Both of Porter's parents were relatively well educated—her father, an unreconstructed Confederate, had been sent to a good military academy, and her mother had been a schoolteacher before her marriage.

When Porter was two, her mother died shortly after the birth of a third daughter, and Harrison Porter moved his young family 140 miles south to Kyle, Texas, a small town where his mother, Catherine Anne Porter, lived. After his wife's death, Harrison Porter was so grief-stricken that he made a number of irresponsible financial decisions that plunged his family into a poverty from which they never emerged.

All her life, Porter suffered from melancholy and depression, probably due in part to the chaotic conditions of her early childhood. From the first, Porter was aware of her family's disgrace and poverty, which were compounded by her father's refusal to do any work that he considered beneath his dignity. The four children were crowded into their grandmother's tiny house, and wore ragged, cast-off clothing. Throughout her life, on the rare occasions when Porter would come into money, she would spend lavishly on her clothes and her appearance.

Harrison Porter grew hostile, drunk, and occasionally violent towards his children. Porter later wrote, "his gloom was so heavy, it seemed to darken the very air around him." Porter's grandmother was a repressive Puritan—an independent, hardworking woman who had raised ten children. "Aunt Cat" Porter's wrath, her granddaughter said, was the only constant thing in her childhood. But the fact that Callie later took her grandmother's name indicates the esteem in which she held the old woman, who inadvertently laid the foundations for her granddaughter's career. Aunt Cat was an inveterate storyteller, whose tales always had a moral point. Porter grew up hearing Civil War anecdotes along with family myths, such as the one reflected in Porter's story "Old Mortality," which was based on tales her grandmother told about Porter's Aunt Annie.

When Porter was eleven, her grandmother died suddenly while the little girl was accompanying her on a trip to visit relatives in east Texas. The Porter family was immediately plunged into chaos. Harrison Porter became even more shiftless, and Callie and her siblings were, for a time, farmed out to various relatives in the area.

The bleakness of her outer world caused Porter to turn inward and develop her imagination. She was quick-witted and rebellious, but an erratic student; her dream was to become an actress. When she was thirteen, her father moved the entire family to San Antonio, where she was to study drama, and borrowed enough money to send Callie and her older sister Gay to a good private school for one year. Her older brother Paul had already joined the navy. At the Thomas School, Callie did poorly, getting mostly D's, except in English, in which she excelled. But she loved the Spanish flavor and outlaw legends of the exotic city, and was thought to be a talented actress by her instructors, who helped her find summer stock work with a local theater when she graduated.

After her year at school, it was left to Porter and her sister Gay to support the family. Harrison Porter next moved his family to Victoria, Texas, a prosperous ranching town, where Katherine—as Callie had begun calling herself—and Gay gave elocution and deportment lessons to local rural women hungry for culture and polish.

At fifteen Porter was an arrestingly pretty girl: A photograph of her that won a local photography contest shows her striking a kittenish pose, her petite curvy figure clothed in a short dress, her long wavy black hair falling over her shoulders, her gray eyes bright. A month after she turned sixteen, she married John Henry Koontz, a twenty-year-old railroad clerk who was the son of a thriving area rancher. The Koontzes were an industrious Catholic family of Swiss descent, headed by a strong father. This structure was at first reassuring, after the disarray of Porter's own family life.

But the youth and sharply differing temperaments of the young people—Koontz was hardworking and stubborn, Porter flighty, spendthrift, and argumentative—doomed the marriage early. The union quickly became unstable and even physically violent.

The young Koontzes lived first in Houston and later, after John Henry took a job as a traveling salesman, in Corpus Christi, a cosmopolitan seaport city on the Gulf Coast. Porter was overjoyed to find that a close childhood friend from Kyle, Texas, Erna Schlemmer Johns, was also living there with her husband. The two renewed their friendship, and Johns would remain a lifelong friend. In a magazine interview given late in her long life, Porter remembered being thrilled by Gertrude Stein's *Tender Buttons*, which she recalled purchasing at a Corpus Christi bookstore. (While it is very likely that she was first exposed to modern literature in Corpus Christi, she could not have first read *Tender Buttons* there—the book wasn't published until 1914, a year after she left the city.) In 1912, she published her own first poem in one of the trade journals her husband subscribed to. Filled with a renewed sense of life's possibilities, Porter, with the moral support and financial aid of her friend Johns, planned to escape her marriage.

Porter left Corpus Christi in 1913, traveling first to Chicago, where she found work as an extra in the fledgling motion picture industry. The work was grueling, and Porter's health was delicate. Within six months she became too weak to continue. But during the long hours under the hot lights, she absorbed the technique of dramatizing a story, and would later apply what she had learned to her own works of fiction.

In a *Paris Review* interview decades later, she said of her early years of teenage marriage and her wandering bohemian life, "I realize now that all that time a part of me was getting ready to be an artist. That my mind was working even when I didn't know it, and didn't care if it was working or not."

In 1914, she returned to Texas, where her sister Gay, pregnant and abandoned by her husband, needed help. Porter went to work in vaudeville to support her sister and her sister's children, singing songs and reading medieval poems on the Lyceum circuit that toured the tiny, rural Texas towns. After her sister's husband returned, and the troubled couple uneasily reconciled, Porter traveled to the town where her own estranged husband was living to file for divorce.

The exertions of the previous few years had taken their toll on Porter's health: In late 1915 she was diagnosed as having tuberculosis. But the misfortunes of Porter's life had a way of turning into opportunities. While undergoing treatment in a hospital in Carlsbad, Texas, she met a fellow patient, Kitty Barry Crawford, who with her husband had cofounded the newspaper the *Fort Worth Critic*. She told Crawford that she had worked as a reporter for *The Dallas Morning News*, and on this basis, the newspaperwoman gave Porter her first writing job—filling in as drama critic while she herself continued recovering. Despite her lack of training, Porter proved to be a speedy and adept writer—she was superb at crafting gushing fashion columns.

In 1918, Porter went to visit Crawford in Denver, Colorado, where she was still recuperating. While there she landed a job on the prestigious *Rocky Mountain News*, and after her friend returned to Texas, Porter stayed on in the western city alone.

It was there in the fall of 1918, amid the combined hysteria of the hate campaign against Germany and the horror of the flu epidemic, that the nightmarish but all-too-true events dramatized in *Pale Horse, Pale Rider* unfolded. While Porter lay ill, her obituary was prepared by her coworkers at *The Rocky Mountain News*, and her family in Texas made arrangements for her funeral. After her unexpected, miraculous recovery, Porter left the hospital stunned by the death of her lover. She had lost all her hair; she had a broken elbow, suffered when she fell after being made to walk too soon; and she had a severe case of phlebitis in her left leg.

Her near-death experience while in a coma, combined with the shock of her lover's death, Porter said, "just simply divided my life, cut across it like that." She later wrote that she perceived that "everything before was just a getting ready" and afterward, she was "alienated, in the pure sense."

Her illness served as a "moment of truth" to cement her desire to become a good journalist and writer. When she returned to her job at *The Rocky Mountain News* in February 1919, her writing changed, becoming more mature and literary, demonstrating a heightened sense of moral insight. In her theater reviews, she condemned the "wicked villain, innocent victim" equation she saw repeated ad infinitum on stage. She wrote that the collaboration of so-called "good people," and their indifference, were the necessary ingredients that allowed the villains of the world to carry out their handiwork. A repeated theme in her future work would be the triangle of villain, victim, and not-so-innocent heroine/hero.

Although inwardly changed, Porter immediately plunged back into life following her illness. She was promoted to drama editor, acted in local productions herself, and was swamped with male admirers. During all this time, her desire to write fiction was germinating. She set her sights on broader horizons, and in late 1919, she left for New York. It was at this time that she wrote her sister of her determination to become a great writer.

In New York, Porter lived a bohemian life in Greenwich Village. She worked for a time in a well-paying position as a movie publicist, but found that the work exhausted her so that she had little time to pursue her fiction. She published at least one story for children in 1920, and her first adult story, "The Adventures of Hadji: A Tale of a Turkish Coffee House," was published later that year in *Asia* magazine. Like many of her later works, it featured a strong woman and a weak man.

Porter fell in with a sophisticated group of people working in New York's literary world, in whose company she felt provincial and untraveled. She felt that to become a good writer, she needed to broaden her base of experience. Through friends she had met in the city, she was appointed correspondent for a Mexican promotional magazine, and spent much of 1920 and 1921 in Mexico City. There she lived among revolutionaries and artists, taught dancing, ventured among the Indians, and sent dispatches of what she saw to the *Christian Science Monitor* and other publications. She ghost-wrote the life story of an American woman she met there who had married a Chinese aristocrat, and in 1921, when she herself was suspected by the Mexican government of being a Bolshevik, fled to her friend Kitty Barry Crawford in Fort Worth. The Crawfords lent her money to return to New York, and there, in her room at 75 Washington Place in Greenwich Village, she wrote her first major story, "Maria Concepción."

This tale of adultery and revenge is based on an actual incident in which a young Indian heroine had murdered her husband's lover, but was protected from the police, both by her repentant husband and by villagers aware of her guilt. The story reflects a deep intimacy with Mexico, examining a woman-focused Indian heritage in conflict with the very male culture of Spanish Christianity. Porter sold the story to *Century* magazine for the staggering sum of $600.

Despite this strong start, the next five years saw little productivity in Porter's fictional output, as she spent much of her time and energy in fruitless romantic pursuits. Now in her thirties, Porter was desperate to settle down to a normal domestic life. Since her divorce, she had had an unending string of affairs, each one leaving her with lowered self-esteem.

In 1922 she returned to Mexico to live for several months, nominally to organize an art exhibit, but also to try to revive a romance. After her return to the United States in 1924, she lived for a time with friends, John and Liza Dallet, who were renting a house in rural Windham, Connecticut. There she tried to concentrate on fiction, but she started far more stories than she finished. Another story set in Mexico, "Virgin Violetta," however, was published in *Century* later that year. That winter she lived with the Dallets in New York, supporting herself by writing book reviews for *The New Republic* and *The New York Herald Tribune*. There she met Ernest Stock, a twenty-five-year-old British aristocrat studying art in New York. They married after a quick courtship, and moved with a group of artist and writer friends to a farmhouse in Connecticut. Among this group was the writer Josephine Herbst, who would become Porter's long-time friend.

Katherine Anne Porter: "It All Happened"

Porter's writing was stymied by her husband, who became sullen and took to drinking, feeling slighted by her devotion to her work. The unhappy atmosphere of this period is captured in Porter's story "Rope," published some years later. Porter left Stock after less than a year.

In the later 1920s she moved to a building on Hudson Street in Greenwich Village near other freethinking women writers, including the Catholic Socialist Dorothy Day and fellow southerner Caroline Gordon. Through Gordon's husband, the poet Allen Tate, she met Robert Penn Warren. Her association with these three southern writers helped her discard the notion that her southern heritage was a liability.

In the spring of 1927 she got an advance from Boni & Liveright, a New York publishing firm, to write a biography of Cotton Mather, the seventeenth-century New England theologian who was in large part responsible for the witch-hunts that darken early American history. She traveled to Salem, Massachusetts, the historical scene of the trials, to research her work. The setting and her subject matter strengthened the literary link Porter had always felt with the early nineteenth-century American writer Nathaniel Hawthorne, who like her was obsessed with the complicity of "innocent" bystanders in the perpetration of evil.

Later that year Porter was witness to a real-life witch-hunt, the Sacco-Vanzetti affair—a notorious trial in which two Italian immigrants were tried for a grisly double murder that took place in the Boston suburb of Braintree, Massachusetts. Because the men were members of a radical anarchist political party, prejudice against the men's nationality and fear of their political beliefs fed the public outcry for their execution. Their cause was taken up by the Communist Party, which won the accused men several appeals before they were finally executed in 1927. Porter attended the final weeks of the trial and was at the vigil outside the prison the night the two were executed, taking copious notes she hoped to form into a book. She was as struck by the Communists' insincerity—their use of the

Italians as martyrs for their own cause—as she was by the hypocrisy of the presiding judges.

The notes Porter took would not become a book for several decades, but the experience helped inspire a fictional work with a related theme, "Magic"—a story about a New Orleans prostitute whose brutalization is facilitated by a host of accomplices. Josephine Herbst submitted the piece to *transition*, an avant garde literary journal, where it was accepted. During this time, Porter also wrote "The Jilting of Granny Weatherall," a portrait of a strong old woman, based on her grandmother.

In early 1928, Porter returned to New York and took a full-time job at a new publishing firm, Macaulay & Company. Through her work there, she met Matthew Josephson, a young author eleven years her junior—he was 27, she 38—who quickly became her lover and mentor. Josephson, who in addition to being a successful biographer was a published poet and a former editor of literary magazines, encouraged Porter to put aside the Mather biography and concentrate on her stories. In 1929 he helped get "Granny Weatherall" published in *transition*. Josephson, however, was married, and when his wife learned of his liaison with Porter, the affair was forced to a close.

Porter's distraught and bereft state of mind at this time is perhaps best expressed in "Theft," a brief but almost perfect story published in the literary magazine *Gyroscope* in 1929, about a woman who is complicit in the losses, both material and personal, in her life. At the story's end, the unnamed protagonist realizes, "I was right not to be afraid of any thief but myself, who will end by leaving me nothing."

Porter became physically ill in reaction to the end of the Josephson affair, and a circle of her friends pooled their resources and sent her to Bermuda to recover and write for several months, sending her money each week. Shortly after her return to New York, when she was living with friends in Brooklyn, she wrote "Flowering Judas," the story that made her literary reputation.

Katherine Anne Porter: "It All Happened"

Its protagonist, Laura, was loosely based on a young woman Porter had befriended in Mexico years before—an idealist aiding the revolutionary cause, stranded between her own Catholic upbringing and her weakening commitment to communism. The girl, through her passive nature, has unwittingly aided in the suicide of one of the imprisoned revolutionaries she is supposed to be helping. The story finishes with a surreal dream in which Laura sees the dead revolutionary accusing her of his murder:

> . . . from the Judas tree he stripped the warm bleeding flowers, and held them to her lips. She saw that his hand was fleshless, a cluster of small white petrified branches, and his eye sockets were without light, but she ate the flowers greedily for they satisfied both hunger and thirst. Murderer! said Eugenio, and Cannibal! This is my body and my blood. Laura cried No! and at the sound of her own voice, she awoke trembling, and was afraid to sleep again.

Porter completed the story in one evening, addressed it to the literary magazine *Hound and Horn*, and walked in the falling snow to mail it at 1:30 A.M. The tale's lyricism and its daring but naturalistic symbolism—the betrayal of Christ alluded to in Laura's eating of the Judas flowers—made the story an immediate sensation. Porter's friends, led by her former lover Josephson, solicited Harcourt, Brace to put out a collection of her stories. *Flowering Judas and Other Stories* came out in a very limited edition of 600 copies in 1930, for which the author received $100.

In 1930 Porter again returned to Mexico and tried to write a novel, but was distracted by her social life. Here she met Eugene Pressly, a Texan thirteen years younger than the forty-year-old author. Pressly would eventually become her third husband.

While she partied in Mexico, her literary reputation grew in New York. She was overjoyed to learn she had been awarded a Guggenheim fellowship, for which friends had encouraged her to apply and had provided recommendations. The $2,000 prize would enable her to travel and live in Europe, a longtime wish. In August 1931 she sailed with Pressly, who was seeking diplomatic work in Europe, on the SS *Wera*, a German ship journeying from Vera Cruz to Bremerhaven, Germany.

Porter took detailed notes on her fellow passengers, many of whom were German, with the immediate intention of writing a novel. But it would take thirty years, another world war and the Holocaust before *Ship of Fools*, the novel this crossing inspired, was completed.

Porter settled in Berlin, where hunger and hardship had been chronic since the end of World War I. Through American journalist friends she met many of the men who were, or would soon become, Adolf Hitler's inner circle. While Pressly was stationed with the foreign service in Madrid, Hitler's henchman Hermann Goering, a widower, served as Porter's escort on more than one occasion. In later years, Porter would exaggerate her association with these Nazis and her recognition of their evil intentions. At the time, she merely took notes, remarking that the Nazi rallies reminded her of the Methodist prayer meetings she'd been taken to as a little girl. She was suspicious of mass hysteria, and found parallels among the Salem witch-hunts, the German-hating frenzy of Americans during World War I, the communism scare of the Sacco-Vanzetti affair, and the national chauvinism she saw rising in Germany.

Through the early and mid-1930s, Porter moved frequently between Berlin, Basel, and Paris, where Pressly was stationed in various diplomatic posts. These were fruitful years for her writing. Europe gave Porter perspective on America, and she began work on stories based on her own childhood, including "Noon Wine" and "Old Mortality." In the mountain atmosphere of the Swiss Alps, reminiscent of Denver, she wrote her first notes for *Pale Horse, Pale Rider*.

Porter and Pressly married in 1933, when Pressly obtained a permanent embassy job in Paris. In 1934, "Hacienda," her long story about expatriates and revolutionaries in Mexico, came out in book form, and the following year an expanded edition of *Flowering Judas and Other Stories* was published. Her stories were now steadily appearing in *The Virginia*

Quarterly Review, *The Southern Review* and other American literary journals.

But as her career star rose, her marriage faltered. Pressly drank and became gloomier the more involved she became in her writing, and she was relieved when his work took him far away. In 1936 the couple finally returned to America, where Porter finished "Noon Wine," staying alone at an inn in Doylestown, Pennsylvania while her husband looked for work in Washington, D.C.

Considered by many critics to be her strongest story, "Noon Wine" is a moral study of a flawed character. The protagonist, Mr. Thompson, is a proud but lazy Texan—not unlike Porter's own father—who commits a murder, for which he is acquitted. But the knowledge of his own guilt weighs on him so heavily that he feels obliged to visit his neighbors, explaining his innocence. At the story's end, unable to convince even himself, Thompson commits suicide.

The bleak setting and tragic tone of this story have their roots in fact, a series of sinister incidents that took place in the rural environs of Buda, Texas, where as a child, shortly after her grandmother's death, Porter was farmed out to live with relatives.

While staying at the Pennsylvania inn, Porter also worked on drafts of "Old Mortality" and *Pale Horse, Pale Rider*, which she had started in Europe, as well as on a story whose working title was "Promised Land," based on her 1931 German crossing. She traveled back to Texas, visiting her family for the first time in twenty years, and in 1937 again settled in New York City. By now she realized that the solitude required for her work would necessitate a divorce from Pressly.

Visiting old friends Allen Tate and Caroline Gordon in the South, Porter met someone who would give further impetus to ending her marriage: Albert Russel Erskine, the twenty-seven-year-old business manager of *The Southern Review*.

Throughout her life Porter was a striking beauty, with a svelte figure and a husky, Texas-inflected speaking voice. Described by some as a femme fatale, she never had trouble attracting the sexual attentions of young men. Erskine fell immediately in love with Porter and quickly pressed marriage, but Porter, in the midst of divorcing Pressly, warned that they would be miserable. Erskine finally wore her down, and in April 1938, the couple married in New Orleans. It wasn't until the ceremony that Erskine learned Porter's real age—he had assumed she was in her mid-thirties, when in fact she was close to fifty—and he was furious. The marriage never recovered from this bad start, and once again, the author found herself living with a man who felt he came second to her work. Nonetheless, they struggled on, and would not divorce for several years.

Porter frequently escaped the claustrophobia of their Baton Rouge apartment by answering the many calls for readings and conferences her blossoming literary reputation garnered. In 1938 she was awarded another Guggenheim fellowship, which she badly needed to support her writing. Literary journals like *The Southern Review*, which published *Pale Horse, Pale Rider* and "Old Mortality" in 1938, and *Story*, which printed "Noon Wine" in 1937, eagerly sought her work, but commercial magazines like *Harper's*, which would have paid well, rejected her. In 1939, *Pale Horse, Pale Rider*, including the two long stories "Old Mortality" and "Noon Wine," was published as a book.

All of Porter's stories, the author claimed, were reportage. "Things have been rearranged, but it all happened, it is all true." *Pale Horse, Pale Rider* is perhaps the author's most dazzling attempt to turn life into literature. The lead character, Miranda, can be read as a surrogate for the author herself, and would appear in several subsequent Porter stories. The short novel first follows the young reporter Miranda over the course of twenty-four hours, just before she succumbs to the flu. The pale rider of the title, symbolizing death, is introduced in an opening dream of Miranda's, and alludes to the fourth horseman of the apocalypse predicted in the Bible, which is pestilence—disease. The influenza epidemic and the war that serve as a backdrop to Miranda's crisis are like manifestations of physical and spiritual illness on earth. The war not only kills, but corrupts: Decadence and cruelty are personified in the war bond salesman who comes to Miranda's office and tries to bully the impoverished young reporter into purchasing a bond, threatening her with firing.

Later, when the play she is assigned to review is interrupted by the hysterical speech of another bond salesman, Miranda sees humanity reduced to an animal state, and looking around at her fellow spectators, thinks:

> *There must be a great many of them here who think as I do, and we dare not say a word to each other of our desperation, we are speechless animals letting ourselves be destroyed, and why? Does anybody here believe the things we say to each other?*

Only with her soldier friend, Adam, does Miranda find intuitive understanding. Yet she fears the love she feels for him, knowing they have no future together—as a soldier, Adam is marked for death. After Miranda returns to her boardinghouse, she becomes ill and delirious. Adam nurses her, but in a series of dreams, she sees their new love as doomed, their world a rotting Garden of Eden, and her lover, like Christ, killed and resurrected again and again. She is taken to a hospital, where she falls into a coma, and where her consciousness "lay like a stone at the farthest bottom of life . . . and there remained of her only a minute fiercely burning particle of being." She experiences a joyous vision of paradise, before being jolted awake and dragged back to life, where the celebrations of the war's end appear nightmarish.

Miranda mourns the heaven she had briefly glimpsed. She opens a letter written by one of Adam's campmates informing her that her lover had been infected with the virus and has died. At the story's end Miranda resigns herself to living in the world, but without really being part of it. She despairs at the irony of returning to this unwanted life for nothing, then feels Adam's presence in the room: "a ghost but more alive than she was." But his spiritual presence is swiftly gone, the room once again silent and empty, and Miranda faces the future alone:

> *No more war, no more plague, only the dazed silence that follows the ceasing of the heavy guns; noiseless houses with the shades drawn,*

empty streets, the dead cold light of tomorrow. Now there would be time for everything.

This very autobiographical story is made universal through its many allusions to the Bible—down to the very name of the sacrificed hero, Adam, who, like his predecessor in the Book of Genesis, is contaminated by knowledge.

The book *Pale Horse, Pale Rider* was published to unanimous high praise for its peerless prose and the depth of human experience the three stories explored. It was awarded the first annual gold medal for literature by the Society of Libraries of New York University in 1940.

That year Porter and Erskine formally separated, and she retreated to Yaddo, a writer's colony in upstate New York, which would be home to her, on and off, for several years. There she wrote many of the stories that would appear in *The Leaning Tower and Other Stories*, published in 1944. Porter, shaken by the fall of France to Nazi Germany and by other dark developments of World War II, drew on her Berlin experiences for the title story about expatriates living in prewar Germany. Several other stories in the collection, subtitled *The Old Order*, show the Miranda character and her relatives during her post–Civil War southern childhood.

After formally divorcing Erskine in 1942, Porter was without a home. Although in a precarious financial position as usual, she longed for a real home of her own, and in 1943 she used the advance she'd received from Harcourt, Brace for the novel about her Atlantic crossing—she was now calling it "No Safe Harbor"—to buy a decrepit country house in Saratoga, near Yaddo. She proved to be no housekeeper, however, and during the one winter she spent there so many things froze and broke in the house that her work suffered. Fortunately, in 1943 she was awarded a one-year appointment as a consultant to the Library of Congress. That year she was also elected a member of the National Institute of Arts and Letters. She thrived in sunny Washington, D.C., boarding with a friend in nearby Georgetown and plunging into an active social life.

One would never guess it from her consistently stylish appearance, but poverty and debt were constants in the author's life until the publication of her award-winning novel, Ship of Fools, *which added riches to her long-established literary fame when she was past seventy. In old age Katherine Anne Porter was honored with nearly every major literary prize, and was a habitué of the Kennedy and Johnson White Houses. A notorious femme fatale, she enjoyed the company of handsome younger men, like her friend and fellow writer Glenway Wescott, pictured here.*
(Library of Congress)

Porter was always a slow writer who had difficulty completing projects. She accepted book review assignments and advance money whenever they were offered, but spent the money before much work was produced. In 1945 she accepted a high-paying job as a screenwriter for Metro-Goldwyn-Mayer in Hollywood, but she was only able to fulfill thirteen weeks of a three-year contract; she was appalled at the low standards of writing to which she was expected to adhere. Her debts pressed her to try again, and she managed to work for a longer stint at another studio, Paramount. All the while she was wrestling with the notes for her novel. Besides the anti-Semitic Germans, other characters populating the novel included a pair of American artists based on herself and Eugene Pressly, a gauche and brutal Texan, a Mexican pimp, and at least two femme fatales, each also partially based on herself. She wrote to Josephine Herbst at this time, "my book is about the constant endless collusion between good and evil . . . I don't offer any solutions, I just want to show the principles at work and why none of us has any real alibi in this world."

Yet Porter herself began to use a heavy-handed moral tone in her dealings with others. In 1947 she and Herbst had a permanent falling-out over a ruthless review Porter had written about Gertrude Stein, in which she pronounced the famous expatriate a phony who had built an undeserved mystique around herself and her work. In the aftermath of World War II, she indulged in the kind of German-bashing she had expressed abhorrence for in *Pale Horse, Pale Rider*. In the late 1940s she made a cross-country college lecture tour, giving speeches that were characterized more by antifascist tirades than by insights into literature. She taught creative writing at Stanford University in 1948–49, and then moved across the country again, settling once more in Manhattan.

At sixty, her next protégé/lover was the thirty-five-year-old Texan writer William Goyen. He would later write of her that "while her writing was full of light, she actually lived in a dark, terrified world that few suspected."

Her great novel, long awaited by her publisher and the literary world, remained unfinished. Instead, *The Days Before*, a collection of previously published literary essays, came out in 1952. In the spring of 1953, worn out by lecturing and hounded by bill collectors, she took a visiting teaching job at the University of Michigan. When she left, the university gave her an honorary doctorate, the first of many. She next traveled to Belgium on a Fulbright teaching grant in 1956. Returning to New York, she was displeased with a change in staff at Harcourt, Brace, and switched to the Atlantic Monthly Press division of Little, Brown in Boston, which gave her fresh advances for all her works in progress.

Finally, in the late 1950s, she rented a house in Connecticut, avoided public life, and attempted to finish her book. In 1958, when the book was "nine tenths done," she ventured out for a few lectures, and received a Ford Foundation grant. In 1959 she taught at Washington and Lee University in Virginia, and she decided to complete her novel there.

A young male friend, her downstairs neighbor in the Georgetown house in which she rented a flat, helped organize the boxes of papers she'd been trailing around the country and to Europe for decades and discovered "Holiday," a story she had written in 1924. She sent it to the *Atlantic Monthly*, where it was published and won an O. Henry award. When John F. Kennedy was elected president, Porter was invited to every inaugural event.

Finally, in June 1961, *Ship of Fools* was completed after twenty-two years of work. Its publication date was set for April 1, 1962, and when it was released, it met with immediate and overwhelming praise. Finally, at seventy-two, she had produced the big book to justify her equally large literary reputation. Her novel was lauded for its panoramic view of individuals struggling with their own limitations, for its mastery at handling several points of view, and for the profundity of the moral questions it raised.

Porter was rich for the first time in her life. She immediately went out and bought a $20,000 emerald ring, and took an extended European holiday with her niece. After the first outpouring of praise, a second wave of more critical reviews appeared, in which the book was faulted for lacking suspense, for being pessimistic, and for its cast of characters, who, although well-drawn, did not grow over the course of the novel. But neither the book's sales nor Porter's reputation were affected. *Ship of Fools* was made into an all-star motion picture, and Porter happily continued to ride the wave of her new fame and prosperity, renting a lavish home in Spring Valley, Maryland.

"If one lives long enough, everything will come," Porter told a cousin at this time. She had achieved everything, except domestic happiness, that she had spent her life striving for. In 1965, Harcourt, Brace came out with *The Collected Stories of Katherine Anne Porter*. The following year, the book was awarded both the Pulitzer Prize and the National Book Award. Porter continued to be showered with honorary doctorate degrees and literary awards, and periodicals both literary and commercial offered high sums to print anything with her byline.

Porter wrote and published very little during the last two decades of her life, but remained an exalted figure in the literary world. She did manage to get her decades-old Sacco-Vanzetti notes organized into a volume, *The Never Ending Wrong*, which was published in 1977. Another volume of non-fiction, *The Collected Essays and Occasional Writings of Katherine Anne Porter*, had come out in 1970.

In extreme old age, the lively garrulousness that had always been part of Porter's personality turned to bitterness, and in her last decade of life she was seized with the same paranoia and dark moods that had plagued her father. She spent her final years in a nursing home in Silver Spring, Maryland, having outlived all of her old friends, enemies, and lovers. She died on September 18, 1980.

Katherine Anne Porter's entire output of fiction is small—twenty-seven stories and one novel—and her reputation rests mainly on the brilliant short stories she wrote in the first half of her life. Critic Edmund Wilson wrote that she produced "English of a purity and precision almost unique in American fiction."

The constant theme running through all Porter's work is the susceptibility of human nature to the corrupting power of evil. Her perspective was that of a traditional Christian moralist; often she examined clashes between old orders, such as governments, religions, and family structures, and the new philosophies and societal forms that replaced them. Underlying much of her work is a sense of a lost birthright, reflecting her experience growing up in a family that had lost its position in the "new" South.

Porter's fiction inspired other American writers who came after her, including Truman Capote, Carson McCullers, and Flannery O'Connor, all of whom explored notions of conflicting orders between the old and new South.

Porter was always angered with biographers and critics who examined her work as a documentation of her life. But there is more of Porter in her fiction than she would have liked to admit to the world. As she once said to her husband Eugene Pressly, "Don't be afraid of giving yourself away, for if you write, you must. And if you can't face that, better not write."

Chronology

May 15, 1890	born in Indian Creek, Texas
1903–5	moves with family to San Antonio; studies drama
1906	marries John Henry Koontz
1913	leaves Koontz; goes to Chicago; works in silent films
1914	returns to Texas; performs on Lyceum circuit
1915	divorces Koontz
1916	gets first journalism job on *Fort Worth Critic*
1918	works as reporter for *Rocky Mountain News* in Denver; stricken with influenza
1919	moves to New York; works as movie publicist and freelance writer
1920–21	travels to Mexico on a writing assignment
1922	publishes "Maria Concepción"
1925–26	marries, divorces Ernest Stock
1930	publishes *Flowering Judas and Other Stories*
1931	receives Guggenheim fellowship; travels to Mexico and then to Germany
1933	marries Eugene Pressly
1937	receives Book-of-the-Month Club award for *Noon Wine*; divorces Eugene Pressly
1938	marries Albert Erskine; receives second Guggenheim
1939	publishes *Pale Horse, Pale Rider*

1940	receives gold medal for literature from Society of Libraries of New York University for *Pale Horse, Pale Rider*
1942	divorces Erskine
1943	elected member of the National Institute of Arts and Letters
1944	*The Leaning Tower and Other Stories* published
1958	receives Ford Foundation grant in literature
1962	publishes *Ship of Fools*, which becomes best-seller; awarded Emerson-Thoreau bronze medal of American Academy of Arts and Sciences; receives O. Henry award for "Holiday"
1965	*The Collected Stories of Katherine Anne Porter* published
1966	*The Collected Stories* awarded Pulitzer Prize and National Book Award
1970	*The Collected Essays and Occasional Writings of Katherine Anne Porter* published
September 18, 1980	dies at nursing home in Silver Spring, Maryland

Further Reading

Porter's Works

The Collected Stories of Katherine Anne Porter. New York: Harcourt, Brace & World, Inc., 1965. The complete stories, including the short novel *Pale Horse, Pale Rider* and stories in *The Old Order: Stories of the South*.

Ship of Fools. Boston: Little, Brown, 1962. The author's epic novel, examining pre–World War II anti-Semitism and other human evils on board a transatlantic cruise ship.

Books About Porter

Bloom, Harold, ed. *Katherine Anne Porter: Modern Critical Views*. New York: Chelsea House Publishers, 1986. Essays by fellow writers and critics analyzing the author's work.

Givner, Joan. *Katherine Anne Porter: A Life*. New York: Simon & Schuster, 1982. The definitive adult biography of the writer.

Lopez, Enrique Hank. *Conversations with Katherine Anne Porter: Refugee from Indian Creek*. Boston: Little, Brown, 1981. Fascinating oral chronicle of the author's life, based on taped conversations.

Zora Neale Hurston
Genius of the South

After a long stretch of wandering, parental abandonment, and near starvation in her native South, Zora Neale Hurston landed in the Harlem Renaissance scene like a meteorite. With only a few stories to her credit, she quickly became a celebrated figure in both black and white literary circles thanks to her extravagant, outgoing personality, her flamboyant clothes, and her daring sense of humor.
(Library of Congress)

When the novelist Alice Walker was a fledgling writer in the 1960s, she searched in vain for an authentic African-American female voice and literary tradition to follow. She finally found what she was looking for in a tattered copy of Zora Neale Hurston's out-of-print 1937 novel, *Their Eyes Were Watching*

God. Curious about the creator of this masterpiece, Walker learned that Hurston was the author of seven books and was the best-known female figure in the Harlem Renaissance of the 1930s, as well as a student of anthropology at Columbia University and a Guggenheim fellow. Why, then, had this vibrant and accomplished woman, who had seemingly transcended so many of her era's barriers, been allowed to slip into obscurity?

The answer to this question is as complex as the woman herself. Genius, feeble, flamboyant, humorous, placating, over-righteous, argumentative, black nationalist, segregationist, Uncle Tom—all of these terms have been applied to Zora Neale Hurston. Hurston produced an eclectic body of work that included anthropology, fiction, drama, and personal memoir. Her seven books were rediscovered in the 1970s by black feminist scholars who valued her wish to find an identity for black people as complete, complex human beings. But her ability to thrive as a writer during her lifetime was limited by the poverty that was nearly endemic to blacks living in America in the early part of this century.

Zora Neale Hurston, the fifth of Lucy Ann and John Hurston's eight children, was born on January 7, 1891, in Eatonville, Florida. John Hurston had risen from being a sharecropper to being a landowning farmer, a preacher, and a carpenter with other men in his employ. He had moved his family to the all-black and newly incorporated town of Eatonville a few years before Zora's birth, attracted to the idea of living in a black-run town, the first of its kind in the United States.

Though Zora's mother had married and begun her family when she was still a teenager, she came from a relatively well-to-do, educated black family. Lucy Hurston embued each of her children—and especially her avowed favorite, Zora—with a strong sense of self-worth, and had drummed into each the principle that education was of paramount importance for success in life. Zora's father did not favor his female children—a fact the author lightheartedly noted in her 1942 autobiography, *Dust Tracks on a Road*: "I don't think he ever got over the trick he felt that I played on him by getting born a girl."

When Hurston was seven, she began to experience visions that portended the arduous, adventurous path her wandering life would take. She recalled in her autobiography, "I knew that they were all true, a preview of things to come . . . I knew that I would be an orphan and homeless . . . that I would have to wander cold and friendless until I had served my time." After the visions began, she said, "I played, fought and studied with other children, but I always stood apart within. Often I was in some lonesome wilderness . . . A cosmic loneliness was my shadow."

The beckoning horizon, and the journey necessary for growth and learning, would be recurrent themes in Hurston's fiction. In her own life the urge "to go places" was first manifested in her childhood habit of hitching rides with white motorists passing through Eatonville—a pastime that earned her a sound whipping when her father learned of it.

Hurston's parents preached differing approaches to survival in a white world. Her mother encouraged her to be strong and outspoken. Zora would write in her 1942 autobiography, "I was impudent and given to talking back, but she [her mother] didn't want to 'squinch my spirit' too much for fear that I would turn out to be a mealy-mouthed rag doll by the time I got grown." Her father advised her to stay out of trouble and to be ever wary of the racism that was prevalent outside of Eatonville. The cocoonlike environment of her native town gave Zora an unshakable sense of self-esteem, inner freedom, and safety. It was this protective upbringing that enabled her to take unusual artistic risks later in life.

Hurston received an excellent education in Eatonville's public school system, which was modeled on principles designed by the black scholar and scientist Booker T. Washington. As a little girl, she liked to invent stories about her surroundings and neighbors. A reclusive old man down the block became king of the alligators at night. She told her mother that she conversed with the tropical birds in her backyard, and with the lake, which asked her to walk on it. In fifth grade, she gave such an impassioned reading of Greek mythology that some visiting white women shipped her a crate of books—the tales of Hans Christian Andersen, Rudyard Kipling, and Robert Louis Stevenson. She loved Greek, Roman, and Norse mythology, and found parallels between the ancient myths and the folktales she heard from her neighbors on the front porch of the local dry goods store.

These stories, sometimes called "lying sessions" by their practitioners, were folktales passed down from slave times and included alternative creation theories, explanations of why people were white or black, and stories featuring talking animals. Hurston would later capture this oral tradition with its humor and imagination in her folklore collection, *Mules and Men*.

When Zora was thirteen, her mother died, and she was sent off to join her older siblings at a "colored" boarding school in the segregated city of Jacksonville. She later wrote in her 1928 essay, "How It Feels to Be Colored Me," "I left Eatonville, the town of the oleanders, as Zora. When I disembarked from the river boat at Jacksonville, she was no more . . . I was a little colored girl."

Yet Zora thrived in her new environment, excelling in all her subjects except math. But at the end of the year, her father did not show up to retrieve her. He had remarried, and his new wife was jealous of his children by his first wife. John Hurston had written to the principal of the school requesting that it "adopt" Zora. Along with her other siblings, Zora was temporarily farmed out to relatives. She eventually returned to Jacksonville, where for several years she led a nearly destitute existence, supporting herself as a maid or waitress, but losing many jobs because of her outspokenness. Of this difficult period she wrote in her autobiography: "My insides tortured me so that I was restless and unstable. I was doing none of the things I wanted to do . . . There is something about poverty that smells like death . . . Dead dreams dropping off the heart like leaves in a dry season . . . People can be slave ships in shoes."

Hurston's exact doings and whereabouts during these years are unclear. Hurston was secretive about this period, obscuring her birth date and simply shaving the ten years off her age. It is known that around 1910 she got a job as a ladies' maid in a traveling operetta company. The position proved to be a lucky break: The young white actress she served became a mentor, encouraging Hurston to read widely and continue her education. Hurston enjoyed traveling with the troupe and learned much that she would use when she staged her own theatrical productions years later. It is estimated that Hurston stayed in this job for two or three years, and that a brief marriage may have impelled her to leave the company. Little is known of her whereabouts after that until 1917, when she enrolled in Baltimore's Morgan Academy, a private high school populated by middle-class blacks. The dean of the school arranged for her to work as a live-in maid in the home of one of the school's trustees, a clergyman whose household had an excellent library.

Shortly after returning to school, Hurston learned that her father had been killed in a car accident. As was typical of her forgiving nature, she put to rest any lingering bitter feelings she might have had about him, instead channeling all her energy into furthering her education. At Morgan she became a popular and outstanding student, quickly completing her course work to graduate in 1918.

After a year at Morgan State College in Baltimore, she entered Howard University, the prestigious black college in Washington, D.C., in 1919. It was a time of rising awareness for African Americans just a few generations removed from slavery and still struggling to establish an American identity. Many blacks had migrated north to work in factories during World War I; others had fought bravely in Europe. Yet most found equality elusive, and segregation and discrimination in wages and housing were standard almost throughout the country. Various black leaders proposed different ways of defeating racism. Booker T. Washington's moderate views, supporting "separate but equal" policies, were opposed by W. E. B. Du Bois, the founder of the National Association for the Advancement of Colored People (NAACP). The latter's views appeared in *The Crisis*, a new magazine Hurston and her Howard friends read and discussed. Two of Hurston's Howard professors, Alain Locke and Montgomery Gregory, advocated black pride rather than assimilation into white culture. In 1920, the year she received an associate degree from Howard, Hurston fell in love with fellow student Herbert Sheen. They planned on marriage, but he left Howard for medical school in Chicago in 1924. Hurston, meanwhile, who had been working her way through college as a manicurist, in 1921 published her first short story, "John Redding Goes to Sea," in *Stylus*, the campus literary magazine. The tale reflects her childhood in Eatonville, exploring the tensions she herself felt in wanting to belong to the nurturing all-black community while also having the urge to explore the world. It was also, on a higher level, an expression of the black experience in predominantly white America.

In 1924 her story "Drenched in Light" was published in *Opportunity* magazine, the organ of the National Urban League. In it, a Hurston-like child from an all-black town hitches a ride with three passing white motorists. The two male passengers dismiss her, but the woman recognizes the child's unique ability to spread light and joy. *Opportunity* editor Charles Johnson was so impressed with the story that he urged Hurston to come to New York. In 1925, she did, claiming second prize for a play, *Color Struck*, in the magazine's annual literary competition.

Hurston hit New York City in the midst of the Harlem Renaissance—a moment when black expression in the arts was flourishing. The movement inspired African-Americans with a sense of pride, heritage, and empowerment, and deeply touched the predominant white culture, from Broadway to the art world to the city's literary salons. Hurston became an immediate star in this milieu. Her colorful clothes, vibrant personality, and riveting storytelling made her an instant celebrity. Her down-to-earth southern sensibility and accent were a contrast to the formal manners of most of the northern-raised and -educated black writers, and Hurston made a striking impression on new friends in the white literary network as well.

White writer Fannie Hurst, who had been one of the judges of the *Opportunity* contest, became Hurston's mentor and friend. She invited the black writer to become her live-in secretary, but when Hurston proved hopeless at the task, she became Hurst's chauffeur instead. At the *Opportunity* awards banquet Hurston also met writer Annie Nathan Meyer, a founder of Barnard College—the women's division of Columbia University—who helped arrange a scholarship for the young writer.

Hurston reveled in the stimulating atmosphere and in her new good fortune, but refused to take this circle of what she saw as sometimes pompous black intellectuals too seriously, dubbing them the "Niggerati," a play on the Latin word for a literary elite, *literati*. Some of her northern-raised black contemporaries accused her of turning herself into a caricature to get whites' attention. The poet Langston Hughes wrote of her, "She was always getting scholarships and things from wealthy white people, some of whom simply paid her just to sit around and represent the Negro race for them."

In 1925, *Opportunity* published a second Hurston story, "Spunk," which involved adultery and supernatural revenge, and which was again set in an Eatonville-like all-black town. The story was included in an anthology published by Hurston's Howard mentor, Alain Locke, called *The New Negroe*.

A new magazine produced under the auspices of this same New York black literary circle, *Fire!!*, which took its title from a Langston Hughes poem, refused to soften its picture of black life for white consumption. Child prostitution and homosexuality were depicted in the journal, as well as Hurston's examination of black color prejudice in her play *Color Struck*, the *Opportunity* award-winner. In 1926 the literary review also published "Sweat," Hurston's story about an unhappily married couple, in which a pious, long-abused wife facilitates her adulterous husband's death. Compared with

Hurston's previous work, the story is marked by a dynamic and mature style, in which elements of folklore and dialect work to great effect. Here men comment critically on their own gender, alluding to the behavior of the story's miserable husband, Syke:

> There's plenty men dat takes a wife lak dey do a joint uh sugar-cane. It's round, juicy an' sweet when dey gets it. But dey squeeze an' grind, squeeze an' grind an' wring till dey wring every drop uh pleasure dat's in 'em out. When dey's satisfied dat dey is wrung dry, dey treats 'em jes lak dey do a cane-chew. Dey thos 'em away. Dey knows whut dey is doin' while dey is at it, an' hates theirselves fuh it but they keeps on hanging after huh tell she's empty—Den dey hates huh fuh bein' a cane-chew an in de way.

Hurston meanwhile had begun her studies at Barnard, where in 1925 she was the only black student. As she sardonically recalls in her autobiography, "The Social Register crowd soon took me up, and I became Barnard's sacred black cow." She began to grow disenchanted with the black literary crowd for what she saw as their overemphasis on the victimization of their race. Any discrimination she experienced astonished her: "How can any deny themselves the pleasure of my company? It is beyond me," she wrote a few years later in her essay, "How It Feels to Be Colored Me."

Hurston began to turn her intellect and energies toward a new discipline. At Columbia, she studied under Dr. Franz Boas, a German-born anthropologist whose ideas ran counter to the then-prevailing view that non-European cultures were "primitive." He encouraged Zora to study her own people.

In 1927 Boas helped her land a scholarship funded by Columbia and the Association for Negro Life and History that enabled her to take a six-month trip to her native Florida and New Orleans. Her mission was to collect as much African-American folklore as possible.

Hurston's research did not go as well as she had anticipated. She had not yet learned to relax and become part of a community of "subjects"—a step essential before she could hope to become their confidante. Discouraged, she took time off from her work to finally marry her college sweetheart, Herbert Sheen. The marriage, which took place in May of that year in St. Augustine, Florida, proved to be a mistake. The relationship was already over, and after a few months the couple lived apart, although they would not divorce for several years.

Hurston next traveled to Mobile, Alabama, to interview Cudjo Lewis, a former slave who had been captured in Africa and shipped to America in 1859. In Mobile Hurston also ran into her New York friend Langston Hughes, who had been visiting the South for the first time, giving poetry readings. The two drove back to New York together. On this car trip they got the idea of collaborating on a play, which would eventually be called *Mule Bone*, to be set in a rural black southern community. When the two writers returned to New York, Hughes introduced Hurston to his patroness, Charlotte van der Quick Mason, a wealthy white woman interested in black folk art and history. In December 1927 Hurston signed a contract with Mason that gave her a $200 monthly allowance for a year of folklore collecting. Hurston was, however, required to give up control over her material, and was prohibited from publishing *anything* without Mason's permission. In addition, the patroness insisted that all her protégés calls her "Godmother." Hurston, who had yet to receive her B.A. degree from Barnard (she would do so the following year), was unqualified to receive further funds from Columbia, and so she accepted Mason's terms in order to continue her research.

She immediately left for Polk County, Florida, a rough backwater logging community. This trip reaped rich folkloric rewards that would later be showcased in her book *Mules and Men*—but only at risk to her life. When the lover of a man Hurston had been learning songs from became jealous, word went out that the visiting anthropologist's life was in danger. Fortunately, Hurston had a protector in a woman friend called Big Sweet. In her book, Hurston re-created the drama of the barroom scene of the intended crime:

> *I was paralyzed with fear. Big Sweet was in a crowd over in the corner, and did not see Lucy come in. But the sudden quiet of the place made*

her look around as Lucy charged. My friend was large and portly, but
extremely light on her feet. She sprang like a lioness.

Hurston fled the bar in the mayhem that followed, and left the logging community soon afterwards. Her next stop was New Orleans, where she researched voodoo, a religion with African roots practiced by some Louisiana Creoles. She even underwent an induction ceremony, during which she experienced what she called "exalted dreams." Hurston remained in New Orleans through the spring of 1929, then traveled briefly to Nassau in the Caribbean. She finally returned north in early 1930 to write up her notes in a house in Westfield, New Jersey, which her patroness had rented for her and Langston Hughes.

There the two writers began work on the play they had discussed years before during their trip back from Mobile. The romantic comedy featured a love triangle—two best friends at odds over the same woman. After the first act of the play was completed, Hurston had a falling-out with Hughes, and left New Jersey. Shortly after that Hughes was dropped by their mutual patroness for publishing a poem she found offensive. He was living with his mother in Cleveland when he learned that a local theatrical group was rehearsing a play called *Mule Bone*, whose book listed a single author—Zora Neale Hurston. The completed play was mainly Hurston's work; unbeknownst to her, it had been passed on to the theatrical troupe by a third party. Hurston refused to give Hughes co-credit; the group dropped the production, and though the play was never produced in Hurston's lifetime, the two writers, unlike the characters in their story, never healed their rift.

In March of 1931, Mason released Hurston from her contract, a release that Hurston welcomed, although "Godmother" would continue to provide sporadic financial backing for several years. Mason funded Hurston's first successful theatrical production, in which her dream of bringing black folklore to the Broadway stage was finally realized. The production, *The Great Day*, concerned life among a group of railroad camp workers, and was staged for a single night in January 1932. Hurston was overjoyed when it won considerable media attention and drew unanimous rave reviews: "The world wanted to hear the glorious voice of my people."

Soon after that, Hurston returned to Eatonville to write up her notes for *Mules and Men*, but was sidetracked by another calling—fiction.

In 1933 she wrote "The Gilded Six Bits," a tale in which greed comes between a husband and wife. When the work was published in the prestigious *Story* magazine, an inquiry from Lippincott, a New York publisher, followed. An editor there wanted to know if Hurston had a novel-length manuscript. Hurston, who as early as 1929 had been thinking about the story that would become the novel *Jonah's Gourd Vine*, moved to Sanford, a small town near Eatonville, rented a one-room house for $1.50 a week, lived on 50 cents a week lent by a cousin, and wrote the book in three months.

The novel, a largely autobiographical work, illuminates the troubled relationship between Hurston's parents, and in richly descriptive language portrays the community of her childhood. Though the father in the story is eventually destroyed by his own pride, regret, and anger, Hurston depicted him in an understanding light.

Two weeks after Hurston had submitted her manuscript to Lippincott, on October 16, 1933, she was evicted from her house for nonpayment of rent. She had meanwhile been working on a new theatrical production called *From Sun to Sun*, to raise some cash. On the day she was evicted, she received a telegram from New York: Her manuscript had been accepted and she would shortly receive a $200 advance.

When it was published, the book was greeted with high praise and was quickly chosen as a Book-of-the-Month Club selection. Hurston's portrait of her troubled father was seen as typical of the powerlessness felt by many black men still deeply conscious of their slave history.

In late 1933, *From Sun to Sun*, later called *Singing Steel*, Hurston's second black folkloric musical production, toured several small Florida towns before being staged in Chicago.

Whites loved the show, but some black critics found it too "darky"—like the minstrel shows that featured blackface characters derisively played by white actors. Hurston was impatient with blacks who simply wished to replicate white art forms. She would later write, "Until we have placed something upon his street corner that is our own, we are right back where we were when they filed our iron collar off."

After this show, Hurston settled down to complete her folklore collection *Mules and Men*, which Lippincott published in October 1935. Hurston's work was again warmly received by white critics, who praised it for its artful blending of anthropological documentary and personal travelogue. While *Mules and Men* fascinated whites, it drew the contempt of many black critics, who accused Hurston of drawing attention to the lowest classes of black humanity, thus encouraging whites to hold on to negative stereotypes. In addition, they said, it wasn't bitter enough about the poverty-stricken condition of southern blacks, who since the onset of the Depression had been subject to a renewed wave of lynchings and beatings at the hands of whites.

In the spring of 1935, Hurston won a Guggenheim fellowship to travel to the West Indies and research folkways and voodoo. She traveled first to Kingston, Jamaica, then lived in the mountains with the Maroons, a community descended from slaves who had fought for and won their freedom in the 1700s. Hurston was especially enchanted by Caribbean music, and immediately began scheming to find a way to bring the joyous, African-influenced rhythms to American theaters.

After six months in Jamaica, Hurston traveled to Haiti, where she took a break from her anthropological research to write her masterpiece. *Their Eyes Were Watching God*, she later admitted, was written in the aftermath of a passionate love affair with a young man she merely refers to in her autobiography as "A.W.P.," a twenty-three-year-old divinity student who adored her. The young man, like many others over the course of Hurston's life, could not comprehend the supreme status that writing held in her life. Her trip to Jamaica, she said,

In later years Hurston's optimistic "color-blind" attitude was at odds with the philosophy of the rising black civil rights movement, which saw restrictions on blacks' freedom and status as rooted in white laws and prejudices. Despite rejection by her colleagues, poor health, and poverty, Hurston never lost her belief in either her own writing or the fundamental goodness of life.
(Library of Congress)

had been made partly to facilitate the ending of the affair. Into her novel, which she wrote in a mere seven weeks, she said she had "tried to embalm all the tenderness of my passion for him."

Their Eyes Were Watching God is the story of one African-American woman's quest for self-realization. This quest takes her through three marriages and on a journey during which she braves physically threatening situations and witnesses mass deaths, and is finally forced into the mercy killing of her last and most beloved husband. The language of the novel is both simple and profound, alternating between the black dialect of the characters and full-blown poetic lyricism. The heroine, Janie Crawford, is guided through the book by a vision of a pear tree she first observes at age sixteen—an image through which she gleans some sense of what a loving relationship between a man and a woman should be:

> *She was stretched on her back beneath the pear tree soaking in the alto chant of the visiting bees, the gold of the sun and the panting breath of the breeze when the inaudible voice of it all came to her. She saw a dust-bearing bee sink into the sanctum of a bloom; the thousand sister-calyxes arch to meet the love embrace and the ecstatic shiver of the tree from root to tiniest branch creaming in every blossom and frothing with delight. So this was a marriage! She had been summoned to behold a revelation.*

Many years pass before Janie realizes in her own life what the beckoning vision promised. After an arranged marriage with a gruff, ugly older man, she elopes with handsome young Jody Starks, an aspiring businessman. Leaving her older husband, she imagines that with Jody, "From now on until death she was going to have flower dust and springtime sprinkled over everything." Yet her dream remains elusive. Jody soon becomes the success he promised to be, but keeps Janie sequestered and silent, treating her like a possession and belittling her in public.

Widowed before her fortieth birthday, Janie next meets and goes off with Tea Cake, an easygoing adventurer several years her junior. With him she slowly gains independence. In their relationship, Janie and Tea Cake restructure social and gender roles—he takes turns with domestic tasks, she learns to hunt and enjoys working in the fields and practicing many "common" pursuits the genteel Jody had disdained. With Tea Cake, Janie achieves full participation in life, including a place in a folk community that allows her to become a storyteller—something denied her by Jody. Her journey is one from passive girl-wife to active maturity. The author shows that the folk communities in which Janie and her various husbands function—like Edith Wharton's high society—can be both nurturing and restrictive.

By the time Janie returns home alone from her journey to tell her best friend Pheoby of her experiences, her romantic image of the pear tree has changed and grown into a full picture representing her own life, with both good and bad elements. To expand this picture, Janie had to journey and endure pain and tragedy, learn about life for herself, not simply take someone else's word. She tells her friend, "Two things everybody's got tuh do fuh theyselves. They got tuh go tuh God, and they got tuh find out about livin' fuh theyselves."

The manuscript of the novel was sent off to Lippincott in December 1936, and when she returned to New York in early 1937, Hurston learned that the publication date had been set for the fall.

The book received almost universal praise from the white literary community. The critic for the *New York Post* said that the lush sensuality of Hurston's prose was on a par with that of the British author D. H. Lawrence. The *New York Times* called it "a well nigh perfect story." Most black critics, however, attacked the book mercilessly. "A minstrel show," scoffed Richard Wright in *The New Masses*, adding that the novel "carries no theme, no message, no thought."

In fact, the book makes many comments throughout on the situation of blacks in America. Looking back at the end, Janie explains to her friend why her grandmother insisted she make a mercenary marriage to a black man with materialistic, essentially white values: "She was borned in slavery times when folks, dat is black folks, didn't sit down anytime dey felt lak it.

So sittin' on porches lak de white lady look lak uh mighty fine thing to her." Janie chose to reject the "white" values of her grandmother and her first husband, Jody, in favor of the free, easy, darker-skinned Tea Cake. Her journey with him took her further and further into the experience of black culture, which can even be seen to be symbolized in the black "muck" of the swamp on which they lived together.

Later critics of the novel, such as Henry Louis Gates, Jr., have held that its theme of a woman looking for self-definition follows a well-established tradition—the same one explored in, for example, Henry James's *Portrait of a Lady*. Janie's situation—that of oppressed wife within a traditional marriage—became a popular feminist literary theme in the 1970s, but such issues were considered irrelevant by most critics of Hurston's day.

Hurston's next book, *Tell My Horse*, the folkloric result of her Guggenheim-funded Caribbean trip, published in 1938, was an uneven collection that met with mixed notices. But she continued to be lauded in other spheres. In 1939, Hurston was awarded an honorary doctorate degree from her first college, Morgan State.

In June of that year she was married again, to Albert Price III, a twenty-three-year-old playground worker from Florida. The union was an instant disaster, but the couple did not divorce until 1943. Typically, Hurston did not dwell on this failure in her personal life, but threw her energies into her work. She hoped with her next endeavor, *Moses, Man of the Mountain*, to produce something to justify herself in black critics' eyes. In this work, she rewrote the Judeo-Christian biblical story in the guise of African, African-American, and voodoo folklore. The characters spoke in black American dialect, reinforcing the parallels between the Egyptian Jews of the story, who had lived long in bondage, and the African Americans who had repeated similar trials so many thousands of years later.

Despite its socially conscious theme, Hurston's unmistakable stamp of optimism was all over the book. "Freedom was something internal . . . All you could do was give the opportunity for freedom and the man himself must make his own emancipation." Such proclamations were bound to deeply irritate the growing black civil rights community, which identified the obstacles to black freedom as laws and customs enforced externally by a prejudiced white society.

The book was hailed by white critics and once more scorned by blacks—Alain Locke, her Howard mentor, called it "caricature." Hurston herself was disappointed with the work artistically, feeling she had not quite accomplished what she had set out to do.

By 1940, Hurston was nationally known but still not rich. Though well-reviewed, her books had always failed to sell widely. In 1941, her publisher, Bertram Lippincott, suggested she capitalize on her personal fame by writing her autobiography. *Dust Tracks on a Road*, published in 1942, was the result. The book is fascinating reading today as much for what it leaves out as for what is included. Her biographer, Robert Hemenway, noted that in the book "she masked her true sentiments in irony, or defused potentially troublesome racial issues with wit, humor and stylistic ingenuity," refusing to describe or explain how she had circumvented the many barriers that institutionalized racism had put in her way.

Predictably, the black literary community assailed the book when it appeared, accusing Hurston of pandering to whites. Critic Arna Bontemps commented, "Miss Hurston deals very simply with the more serious aspects of Negro life in America—she ignores them."

The larger reading public, both black and white, loved the book, which won the Ansfield-Wolf award from the *Saturday Review of Literature* for its "contribution to the field of race relations." In an interview in the *New York World Telegram*, Hurston defended the "raceless" stance of the book, commenting, "I don't see life through the eyes of a Negro, but those of a person."

In 1943 she moved to Daytona Beach, Florida, and bought a houseboat, fulfilling a lifelong dream. "I have the solitude I love," she wrote in a letter to a friend. On the *Wanago*, she cruised up the Indian and Halifax rivers, docking at various spots for stretches of writing. That year she also received a Distinguished Alumni award from Howard University. During these years Hurston took advantage of her byline's popularity by publishing journalism that clarified her opinions on race relations—including many pieces that strongly denounced the "Jim Crow" laws that enforced segregation.

Several related factors resulted in a decline in Hurston's literary output in the 1940s. The first was lack of money. In the 1930s and 1940s, black writers did not receive large advances, because publishers did not anticipate large audiences for their work. If their books were not about the "race problem," they seldom sold well. Of Hurston's colleagues, only Richard Wright and Langston Hughes made a living exclusively from their writing.

Finding a voice that was acceptable to both black and white audiences was her major problem. In the 1940s, the picture of blacks acceptable to northern liberals was the one Richard Wright drew in his novel *Native Son* (1940), which showed how a racist society had turned the young black hero into a pathological monster. Hurston rejected this picture, and attacked the "arrogance" of whites who assumed that "black lives are only defensive reactions to white actions."

In 1945 Hurston suffered from an intestinal illness that had first struck her in Haiti and would continue to plague her for the rest of her life. That year, Lippincott rejected the novel she submitted, "Mrs. Doctor," claiming that her literary powers had diminished. Hurston felt that it was the subject matter of the book—upper-class blacks—that was unacceptable to the publisher. Later, in an essay she published in 1950 called "What White Publishers Won't Print," she expressed her frustration at white society's insistence on propagating a narrow view of blacks.

In 1946, she moved back to New York, where she worked for Grant Reynolds, a conservative Republican running for a seat in Congress from Harlem. Reynolds lost, but she remained in

New York, impoverished and depressed, until her next project was organized. Enlisting the influence of fellow Florida writer Marjorie Kinnan Rawlings, she sold the rights to her next and as yet unwritten book to Charles Scribner's Sons. With a $500 advance, she sailed to Honduras, where she hoped to find a lost Mayan city. Her interest in the expedition waned, and instead, while in Puerto Cortes, she wrote another novel, *Seraph on the Suwanee*. Interestingly, she took as her subject the troubled marriage of a pair of rural white southerners. Scribner's bought the manuscript, and Hurston returned to New York to see her book published in 1948.

Almost simultaneously with the book's publication, disaster struck—Hurston was implicated in a child sex scandal. In 1946, she had been rooming in the Harlem house of a woman who had a young son. The child, who was mentally disturbed, had accused Hurston (who had been out of the country at the time) and two other adults of molesting him. On September 13, 1948, Hurston was arrested on a charge of committing an immoral act with a child. Scribner's immediately hired a lawyer and the charges were quickly dropped, but the damage had been done. Though the white press ignored the false charge, not considering the accusation newsworthy, the black papers had a field day, blasting headlines of Hurston's arrest adjacent to racy excerpts from her new novel.

For the first time in her life, Hurston admitted to being devastated. She wrote to her friend, the photographer Carl Van Vechten, "I care nothing for anything anymore . . . My race has seen fit to destroy me . . ."

Her new novel sold well, though the critics agreed that it was not her strongest work—she had failed to bring these white characters truly alive. Scribner's gave her a $500 advance on her next book, and this money became her sole support, outside of sporadic journalism, for two years.

In 1950, Hurston was cleaning house for a wealthy white Miami matron when her employer saw her maid's byline in the *Saturday Evening Post*. A *Miami Herald* reporter somehow got wind of the story, and it wasn't long before the distinguished author's employment status was in the national news. First she claimed to be working as a maid in order to research a character; to other reporters she evasively explained, "A writer has to stop writing now and then and just live a little."

Hurston quickly left her position and moved to Eau Gallie, Florida, where she eked out a living as a freelance writer while working on her next book, a dramatization of the life of King Herod. According to neighbors who knew her then (but did not know that she was a famous writer), Hurston was happy living a simple life and enjoyed tending her beautiful garden. In 1955 Scribner's rejected the manuscript for "King Herod"—a blow that was compounded the following year when the house she had been living in was sold, forcing her to move. Despite these setbacks, Hurston was not a completely forgotten figure. In 1956 she was recognized by Bethune Cookman College in Daytona Beach, where she had briefly taught years before, with an award for "education and human relations." In 1957 she worked as a librarian at Patrick Air Force Base in Cocoa, Florida, then moved to Fort Pierce, Florida, where she worked as a substitute teacher in 1958.

Through these years she continued laboring over the King Herod manuscript and sent regular but unfruitful queries to publishers. Hurston's time seemed to have come and gone; she had lost the world's ear. Having abandoned her best subject matter—the black community and its folklore—and having lost the audience for it, she seemed incapable of convincingly executing work in any other genre. *Seraph on the Suwanee* turned out to be her last published book.

Deteriorating health was another obstacle to her writing. Hurston was solicited to do some journalism for local newspapers, but the work she produced was so fractured that a *Miami Herald* editor commented that he assumed her previously published books had been ghostwritten.

In 1959 Hurston suffered a stroke, and in October of that year she entered the St. Lucie County welfare home, where she died of a heart attack on January 28, 1960. Hurston's former Fort Pierce neighbors paid for her funeral, but her grave, in a segregated Fort Pierce cemetery, was left unmarked. As was her lifelong custom, the author had never informed her surviving family members of her ill health or poverty. Consequently, no tombstone was ordered. In 1973, Alice Walker searched for and found Hurston's grave, then paid to erect a tombstone herself.

For an epitaph, Walker had engraved on the modest monument:

Zora Neale Hurston
"A Genius of the South"
Novelist   Folklorist
Anthropologist

Walker was largely responsible for the movement that brought Hurston's books back into print, introducing them to a new generation of readers and scholars. *Their Eyes Were Watching God*, now recognized as a masterpiece, is widely taught in high schools and colleges across the country today.

Since 1989, the Zora Neale Hurston Festival of the Arts and Humanities, held each January in Eatonville, honors the author's life and works, celebrating the folklore tradition she cherished with plays, readings, and a scholarly conference.

Modern black writers, including June Jordan, Larry Neal, Addison Gayle, Gloria Naylor, Toni Cade Bambara, and Julius Lester, as well as Alice Walker herself, are among those who testify to Hurston's influence. Her unashamed use of black vernacular speech, her inclusion of black women's stories in a genre almost universally male-focused, and above all, her presentation of black characters not simply as victims of white society, but as thriving individuals with a sense of "racial health," are all building blocks for today's expanding chorus of African-American literary voices.

Chronology

January 7, 1891	born in Eatonville, Florida
1904	attends boarding school in Jacksonville
1917	attends Morgan State Academy in Baltimore
1920	receives associate degree from Howard University
1921	first story, "John Redding Goes to Sea," published
1924	second story, "Drenched in Light," published in *Opportunity* magazine
1925	moves to New York City; wins fiction prize sponsored by *Opportunity;* enrolls in Barnard College
1926	begins anthropological studies with Dr. Franz Boas
1927	travels to Florida on first folklore researching trip; marries Herbert Sheen
1928	graduates from Barnard
1931	divorces Sheen
1932	produces the musical *The Great Day* in New York City
1934	first novel, *Jonah's Gourd Vine*, published
1935	folklore collection, *Mules and Men*, published; travels to Jamaica and Haiti to study folkways
1937	*Their Eyes Were Watching God* published
1938	folklore collection, *Tell My Horse*, published

1939	marries Albert Price; publishes novel *Moses, Man of the Mountain*
1942	publishes autobiography, *Dust Tracks on a Road*
1943	divorces Price
1947	travels to Honduras
1948	arrested on false morals charge; publishes *Seraph on the Suwanee*
1951	moves to Eau Gallie, Florida
1955	publisher rejects manuscript for novel, "King Herod"
1959	suffers stroke; enters St. Lucie County welfare home
January 28, 1960	dies in Fort Pierce, Florida

Further Reading

Hurston's Works

Dust Tracks on a Road. Urbana and Chicago: University of Illinois Press, 1984. This new edition of Hurston's 1942 autobiography includes several chapters excised from her original manuscript, as well as an introduction by her biographer, Robert Hemenway.

I Love Myself When I Am Laughing . . . & Then Again When I Am Looking Mean and Impressive: A Zora Neale Hurston Reader. Edited by Alice Walker. Old Westbury, N.Y.: The Feminist Press, 1979. An anthology of excerpts from Hurston's major works; includes several essays and short stories as well as Walker's essay "Looking for Zora," which details her pilgrimage to Hurston's birthplace and grave site.

Their Eyes Were Watching God. New York: Harper & Row, Perennial Library edition, 1990. The reissue of the classic 1937 novel features a foreword by Mary Helen Washington and an afterword by Henry Louis Gates, Jr.

Books About Hurston

Gates, Henry Louis, Jr., and K. D. Appich. *Zora Neale Hurston: Critical Perspectives Past and Present.* New York: Amistad, 1993. Criticism and interpretation of the author's works, both historical and current, often from feminist and African-American perspective.

Hemenway, Robert. *Zora Neale Hurston: A Literary Biography.* Urbana: University of Illinois Press, 1977. The first definitive investigative adult biography of the author in the context of her time and place.

Witcover, Paul. *Zora Neale Hurston.* New York: Chelsea House, 1991. An excellent biography for young adults, with lively photographs capturing Hurston and her Harlem Renaissance milieu. With a foreword by Coretta Scott King.

Pearl Buck
Writer of Two Worlds

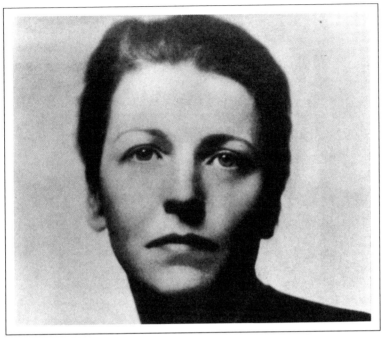

Pearl Buck's altruistic missionary upbringing inspired her pioneering humanitarian work in international relations, civil rights, and women's rights. The author of more than 100 books, she is best known for The Good Earth *and the other books about Chinese life and culture for which she won the Nobel Prize in 1938.*
(Library of Congress)

*T*he turn-of-the-century China in which Pearl Sydenstricker Buck grew up was a strife-torn place, where an ancient aristocratic regime was pitted against a rising class of peasants and industrial workers. As a child exposed to the rough-and-tumble streets of Chinkiang, Buck saw poor families sell their daughters into prostitution in the houses of the rich. As a teenaged missionary volunteer, she met many who had escaped this life, and witnessing their suffering made young Pearl vow to combat cruelty wherever she found it. By the time she reached sixteen, Buck had made two solemn vows to herself: to write novels, and to help the oppressed everywhere. Over the course of her extraordinary life, the fame and fortune engendered by her first goal made the second one possible.

Pearl Sydenstricker was born in Hillsboro, West Virginia, on June 26, 1892, while her Christian missionary parents, Absalom and Caroline, were home on leave from their post in China. Pearl was the fifth child born into the family, but only the second to survive. Between the birth of her brother Edgar, twelve years her senior, and her own birth, two sisters and one brother had died in China of tropical disease, and a younger brother would follow suit.

When Pearl was an infant of three months, she traveled to China with her family. As a small child she was taught by her mother—mainly stories of the Bible and American history. Chinese culture was absorbed through stories told by her nurse, Wang Amah, who would become a model for many of the Chinese peasant characters who would later populate her books.

A tragedy—the death of Pearl's younger brother Clyde at age five—led to her first appearance in print at the age of six, a letter to the editor that appeared in the American religious newspaper *The Christian Observer*: "I have two little brothers in heaven . . . and on the tenth of last month, my brave little brother, Clyde, left us to go to our real home . . ." Pearl's mother urged her to write every day, and several of her pieces appeared in the English-language newspaper the Shanghai *Mercury*, where she won several of the children's writing contests the paper sponsored. There were few Westerners living in the city of Chinkiang, and such English-language newspapers were an important source of contact with the outside world for the isolated American community.

Pearl Buck: Writer of Two Worlds

Lonely after her older brother Edgar was sent to America to attend college, Pearl relied on books for company. Her choice of favorite novel, *Oliver Twist* by Charles Dickens, suggests an early sensitivity to cruelty and injustice. In 1900 a younger sister, Grace, was born; that year also brought violence to China with the Boxer Rebellion, when the poor rose up to protest foreign occupation of their country. One day Pearl's father came home covered in blood after a harrowing incident in which he had been kidnapped and forced to witness a fellow missionary's torture. Pearl, her mother, and younger sister went to Shanghai for a year until the situation calmed down.

Soon after they returned to Chinkiang, Pearl's education was supplemented with lessons from a tutor, Mr. King, a Confucian scholar who introduced her to ancient Chinese philosophy. In addition to volunteering at the Door of Hope mission, at this time Pearl was also helping her parents in their Christian missionary work aiding beggars, lepers, and prostitutes.

Determined to obtain a good education, Pearl had longed to attend Wellesley College in Massachusetts, but family finances and pressure to live near her married brother persuaded her to settle for Randolph-Macon College in Lynchburg, Virginia. After spending a year at a Christian boarding school in Shanghai, Pearl set off with her family on the long trek to her native land in 1911. The Sydenstrickers chose to travel from China across Russia, giving Pearl the opportunity to visit Europe before crossing the Atlantic Ocean to attend college. The poverty she witnessed in prerevolutionary Russia, she later wrote in her 1954 autobiography, was worse than anything she had seen in China or had seen since. She had a premonition that many innocent people would suffer when the anger of the world's outraged people exploded into violence. Her father agreed, rightly predicting that the uprising would begin in Russia and would spread to other countries of Asia, leading to a major conflict between East and West during which Asia's poor would revolt against their long history of colonial domination.

Randolph-Macon was an enclave of southern belles, where Pearl stood out as a dowdy misfit in her missionary-plain clothes, with her hair pulled into a severe bun. In an effort to fit in, she divided her life into what she called "separate worlds." She strove to conform outwardly, altering her clothes and piling her long fair hair into the trendy voluminous pompadour worn by the other girls. Outgoing and naturally friendly, Pearl grew popular and excelled in her schoolwork—though she hated math and Latin—and quickly became a student leader. Though she learned to shine in this superficial milieu, she never lost her concern for nobler causes, and was disappointed to find that when invited to visit the homes of classmates, even their parents lacked the slightest curiosity about her life in China or events outside the United States.

By her sophomore year, Pearl was settled enough to resume writing, and as she did, she began to accumulate literary prizes. During her junior year she served as president of her class, and she graduated with distinction in 1914. She decided not to return to China immediately, instead accepting a post as assistant professor of psychology at her alma mater. But when she learned that her mother was gravely ill with sprue, an incurable tropical disease, she made plans to return to her family. Travel was restricted, since World War I had just broken out; Pearl feared this was the beginning of the great East–West crisis she had foreseen.

While still in the United States, Pearl secured a teaching post in China through the Presbyterian Board of Foreign Missions. A shipboard romance with a young Standard Oil executive on her journey over nearly led to marriage, but Pearl decided that her first duty was to her mother, and to her beloved China.

Once in China, she poured all her energies into nursing her mother and teaching the poor, politically active young Chinese men who were her students. She also took on her mother's missionary responsibilities, acting as a social worker to the local Chinese women.

Meanwhile, political strife in China was escalating. The corrupt dynasties that had ruled China for centuries were crumbling, and the Dowager Empress of the Manchu Dynasty was in exile. In 1912, Nationalist leader Sun Yat-sen had been elected provisional president of the first Republic of China. Under the new republic, society was rapidly changing, with the masses of workers and peasants taking a greater role in government and society. Traditional practices, such as polygamy and female footbinding, were outlawed. Literacy was on the rise, and new magazines offered forums for political exchange. For the first time, Pearl was able to read many English-language publications previously banned or unavailable in China.

Much as the future of China interested Pearl, in her early twenties she was being forced to focus on her personal life. All of her Chinese friends her age, and most of the few American girls she knew, were already married. Pearl enjoyed dating young American men from the diplomatic and commercial community, but this was considered scandalous in her family's conservative missionary circle. Devoted though she was to helping others, Pearl felt the need to break away from her family and establish an independent life.

While spending the summer with her mother in the mountain resort of Kuling in northern China, she met a young man who seemed to offer a bridge to the future. Lossing Buck was a young missionary, the exact same age as Pearl, a graduate of Cornell Agricultural College who had come to bring Western farming methods to China. Theirs was not an intensely romantic attraction, but rather one based on shared goals—a strong desire to help the Chinese and alleviate ignorance and suffering. The Sydenstrickers objected to Buck as a husband for their daughter on the grounds that he was entirely lacking in literary interests and sensibility, which they predicted Pearl would find suffocating over time.

Although Pearl knew that she wanted neither the narrow missionary life nor the isolation of the northern outpost of Nansouchou that marriage to Buck would entail, she agreed to marry him. She later wrote that she did so against her best judgment, but at twenty-five, her need to establish herself in an adult life apart from her family overrode her doubts. The couple married on May 30, 1917.

After a short honeymoon in the Sydenstrickers' stone cottage in Kuling, the young couple settled down to a life of work in Nansouchou. When Lossing concluded that the Western agricultural technology he had brought was useless in China's damp climate, Pearl suggested he make a thorough study of Chinese farming methods instead. The results established Lossing Buck's reputation in his field. In her new life Pearl at first had no time for literary pursuits. She would later write of this period, "I knew of course that I would be a writer, but I was not ready yet." She felt that no writer should attempt a novel until the age of thirty, but should first live life "at full tilt" for nothing but the experience itself.

Buck threw herself into setting up house and into her social work with the unschooled, impoverished and ill women of the community. She saw aspects of the Chinese that appalled her—crime, opium addiction, and the killing and selling of girl babies proliferated in this poor rural region. In a letter to a friend at this time she described China as "a country given to the devil." The peasant women were virtual slaves to their men, and were at the mercy of a culture that valued them only for their labor or their beauty. Yet Buck found much in these hardy females to admire; their humor and courage would be detailed in her later books.

Despite her frequent despair at their living conditions, Buck was well-loved by the women, who christened her "learned woman," or "wise mother." Still Buck was not sorry to leave the desolate region when her husband was appointed to a position at Nanking University, in the heart of that vibrant central Chinese city. Soon after they moved there, in March 1918, Pearl gave birth to a daughter, Carol.

Happy though she was to be a mother, illness followed the birth, and the Bucks were forced to travel to New York, where Pearl underwent surgery to remove both her appendix and a benign tumor. Buck was stricken to learn at twenty-eight that she could have no more children. Back in Nanking, Pearl engaged a Chinese nurse to look after her baby, and resumed teaching. She was well positioned to observe the changing times. At Nanking University, she taught upper-class young men, while at a local government institution she taught the sons of poor workers—the newly literate working class.

Meanwhile, Caroline Sydenstricker was severely ill, and Buck made frequent visits to her in Chinkiang. After her mother's death in 1921, Pearl took her seventy-year-old father and her twenty-one-year-old sister Grace into her own home. In addition, the Bucks hosted a constant stream of guests—professors, visiting Americans, and local intellectuals. Busy as she was during these years, Buck managed to carve out time for writing, most often late at night or early in the morning. Her first major work, which would not see print for many years, was a biography of her mother describing her arduous life; it was eventually published as *The Exile*. Buck made no attempt to publish this work after its completion, but concentrated on her many family duties. But she never forgot her goal. "All those years, while my hands were busy," she later wrote, "these novels have been making themselves in my head."

In the early 1920s, China was ideologically polarized. The north leaned toward restoration of a monarchy bolstered by warlords, while the south supported the democratic future of Sun Yat-sen's progressive Nationalist Party. Following World War I, the Nationalists adopted the Communist philosophy, and riots, student rebellions and worker strikes swept the southern cities. When the smoke cleared, a new leader, Chiang Kai-shek, emerged as the head of the Nationalist Party.

Like many in the university community, the Bucks supported the Nationalist movement as the way to a modern, productive future. During these tumultous years, Pearl was stimulated by the ideological debate that dominated Nanking's intellectual life, and was inspired to begin writing her first novel in secret. However, she was distracted by a new trouble: There was something wrong with her daughter Carol.

Carol was far behind other children her age in development. Buck took her to the United States in 1924 when she and

Lossing took their sabbaticals to earn master's degrees from Cornell. After visits to a host of doctors—which Pearl financed with the timely sale of an essay and a short story—her worst fears were confirmed: Carol was mentally disabled. Doctors advised Buck to promptly institutionalize her daughter, but she refused, choosing instead to add another focal point to the family by adopting another child, a three-month-old girl she named Janice.

When the Bucks returned to China in 1925, Chiang Kai-shek was fighting the northern warlords, attempting to unify the country under his party. Nanking, midway between northern and southern China, was in a particularly vulnerable spot. Although American missionaries were warned to leave, the Bucks stayed.

The Bucks had always considered themselves safe in China, especially since they were informally allied to the Nationalist cause. This sense of security was abruptly shattered on March 24, 1927, when Nationalist troops marched into the city of Nanking. They rioted, looted, and killed Westerners at random, including the vice president of Nanking University. The Bucks' lives were saved by Madame Lu, a Chinese servant who hid them in the tiny shanty where she lived in the alley behind their residence.

Buck later cited this life-threatening event as a turning point in her literary life. At thirty-five, she was trapped in a lackluster marriage, and had made only the most sluggish of starts in her writing career. This jolting experience made her view her previous existence "as if I had spent my life in jail . . . a queer submerged sort of state." While in hiding she vowed that if she lived through that terrible day, she would make a new life.

Fortunately, American military forces came to the rescue, and the Bucks were evacuated to the safe haven of Shanghai. They had lost their home and all of their possessions—including the manuscript of Buck's first novel. The family continued to wait out the conflict in Japan, where Buck, free of teaching responsibilities, was able to do more writing. Here she wrote the first draft of a story called *The Big Wave*, which was about the effect of a tidal wave on a Japanese village. Far from being filed away as a terror to be surmounted and forgotten, Buck's witnessing of the shocking upheaval in Nanking, euphemistically termed the "Nanking Incident" in history books, was stored for later use in the fledgling writer's memory. The scenes of rioting and plunder would later figure in her most famous novel, *The Good Earth*.

The Bucks returned to Shanghai for a year, and Pearl plunged into the city's vibrant intellectual life and began making contacts that enabled her to sell more of her essays and stories to English-language publications. A young poet, Hsu Tze-mo, offered her inspiration and encouragement. Buck found the courage to write to American literary agents overseas, but the first she contacted wrote back that no one in the United States was interested in reading about China. The second agent she approached, David Lloyd, asked to see her work. She sent off a draft of a novel and forgot about it for several months.

When the Bucks returned to Nanking, the atmosphere was still threatening enough to convince Pearl that their days in China were numbered. In advance of an eventual permanent move to the United States, she decided to place Carol in an institution there. Coincidentally, Lossing was awarded a grant to work at Cornell, and the family set sail. Buck placed her daughter in the Vineland Training School in New Jersey, and scrambled for a way to pay the $1,000 annual fee. She obtained a grant from the Presbyterian Foreign Missions Board to write a book, titled *The Young Revolutionist*, which glorified the role of Christian missionaries in China. Concurrently, her agent informed her that the twenty-ninth publisher to whom he had sent Buck's manuscript, the John Day Company, had accepted her novel. Buck, who had been desolate at the separation from her daughter, was now filled with hope.

Titled *East Wind, West Wind*, Buck's first novel, published in 1930, chronicled the life of a Chinese woman trapped in an unhappy marriage. Unquestionably, the work reflected elements of the author's own life, for over time, the Sydenstrickers' predictions had come true. Pearl, an artist at heart, felt deeply alone in her marriage to the singularly practical workaholic Lossing Buck. After Lossing's tenure at Cornell was completed, the Buck family returned to China. The sales of Buck's book had not only earned enough to pay Carol's school tuition for several years, but the luxury for her to stop teaching and devote herself to writing full time. Her next novel, called *The Mother*, concerned the life of a typical Chinese peasant woman, and was based on Madame Lu, the servant who had hidden the Bucks during the perilous Nanking Incident.

Buck's next literary endeavor was a book about the rise of a poor Chinese peasant struggling against a range of obstacles that included war, revolution, famine, and natural disaster. Richard Walsh, Buck's publisher at John Day, came up with the title for the epic story: *The Good Earth*.

Since Buck's previous two novels had been only moderate sellers, and since *The Good Earth* concerned an alien culture and was written in a rather repetitive, biblical style, its smashing success was as unlikely as its protagonist's ultimate triumph over the chaotic conditions of twentieth-century China. When it was published in 1931, *The Good Earth* was chosen as a selection of the Book-of-the-Month Club, and quickly outsold its first printing of 40,000. Buck had an invaluable supporter in Walsh, who in addition to providing tireless encouragement to the author, aggressively promoted the work. He had good reason to—John Day was a floundering, start-up enterprise, and Buck was his best bet among only a handful of writers. The publisher had nearly everything riding on the success of her book. To promote sales, Walsh nominated *The Good Earth* for a Pulitzer Prize.

Fired by this unexpected but long-awaited victory, Buck set quickly to work on a sequel, *Sons*, which continued the family saga of Wang Lung, *The Good Earth*'s protagonist. While members of Buck's missionary circle condemned *The Good Earth* for the frankness with which it portrayed the sexual vices of Chinese men—fearing that it would discourage Americans from continuing to fund their work—the book-reading public heralded it. MGM won a fervid movie rights bidding war, and the book was also adapted for the stage.

Buck was generous with the financial rewards that stemmed from her new literary success: When the Yangtze River flooded, killing 25 million and causing widespread disease, homelessness, and starvation in China, she donated money and publicized the need for further contributions to aid disaster relief.

In 1932, *The Good Earth* was awarded the Pulitzer Prize. During the previous year, it had sold two million copies. To Buck, still living in China with her family, such a stellar achievement seemed almost unreal, coming at age forty after a life of self-sacrifice, privation, and obscurity. There was a tremendous clamor in the United States, both for more Buck books and for her actual presence. That opportunity was at hand, since Lossing Buck had decided to return to Cornell to complete a Ph.D. The first thing Buck did with her new riches on arriving in the United States was to establish a trust fund for her daughter Carol, and endow her school. Buck found that she was an instant celebrity, constantly in demand for public appearances and newspaper interviews, and was quickly awarded honorary degrees from Yale University and her alma mater, Randolph-Macon. In 1936 she was elected to the National Institute of Arts and Letters. Buck basked in the adulation emanating both from her readers and her publisher, Richard Walsh. When *The Good Earth's* sequel, *Sons*, was published, it was to further critical acclaim.

Having lived mainly in China, and having been surrounded throughout her life by idealistic missionary workers, Buck had always harbored a vision of America as a benevolent, civilized, and just place. Once celebrity exposed her to a wider spectrum of life in the United States, she became disillusioned. As a child, she herself had experienced race prejudice—taunted for her blue eyes and fair skin and excluded from games, she had shouted at her tormenters, "I'm just as Chinese as you are!" Seeing America during its darkest depression, when all of the nation's faults and dysfunctions flared up, Buck was appalled at the specter of blatant and prevalent racism, and followed Eleanor Roosevelt's lead in speaking out publicly against it as an abomination contrary to all Christian principles.

When her husband's Ph.D. was completed, Buck accompanied him to China, but the couple, whose marriage had long been an awkward, cumbersome, though respectful, alliance, soon filed for divorce. Lossing Buck was devoted to his missionary work, and to China. Pearl wanted to be in the United States, near her daughter Carol, and in the center of the whirlpool of her newly won literary fame. She also had a new love interest. Her publisher, Richard Walsh, though married with a family of his own, had been proposing repeatedly.

The turmoil in Buck's personal life stalled her fiction output. She revived her very first book, the one about her mother's life, and when published in 1936 under the title *The Exile*, it was warmly received by the reading public. Buck took up an editorial post at John Day and continued the story of Wang Lung's family in *A House Divided*, published in 1936.

That year, Buck and Walsh obtained divorces from their respective spouses, and they were married on June 11 in Reno, Nevada. Soon after the marriage, they bought a country home in Bucks County, Pennsylvania, and the author settled down to work on a biography of her father. She called it *Fighting Angel*, and it added another success to her store of titles. She and Walsh adopted two more children, newborn baby boys they named Richard and John. Her next book, *This Proud Heart*, was about a woman artist, a sculptor whose genius and work were undermined and undervalued by her husband and family. The book was a critical failure—it was, in fact, written in a sentimental, clichéd style appropriate for mass market women's magazines—but women across the nation responded strongly to the work, quickly making it a best-seller. They also flooded the author with an avalanche of letters claiming that Buck had written their own life stories. Buck's fiction and essays were increasingly popular with this audience. Literary snobs criticized her for publishing in forums like *The Ladies'*

Home Journal; she defended herself by saying that promoting understanding between the races and sexes in a forum that reached three million readers was nothing to be scoffed at.

Green Hills Farm, her Pennsylvania home, grew with the addition of two more children—bringing her total brood to five—but in 1937, the author suffered a blow when her older brother unexpectedly died of a heart attack. *The Good Earth* was meanwhile being filmed in China, but the project was sabotaged by the Nationalists, who objected to its depiction of famine and vice. They got hold of and destroyed much of the film, and most of it had to be reshot in the United States.

All of these setbacks were dwarfed in significance when in 1938 Buck received an entirely unexpected honor: the Nobel Prize. She was the second woman to have been so honored, but the first American woman, as well as the first woman to have won both the Pulitzer and the Nobel. She traveled to Sweden to receive the prize from that nation's king, and in her acceptance speech lauded the United States' and China's shared love of freedom.

The years between 1939 and 1945, when World War II raged, were highly productive ones for Buck. She produced ten novels, as well as a stream of articles, essays, and children's books on China. She lectured widely, often speaking on racial equality and women's rights. She sometimes appeared publicly with Eleanor Roosevelt, the First Lady who was renowned for her humanitarian work.

Buck's missionary upbringing had always made her regard the suffering of the world as her personal responsibility, and now she was worried about China, then in a state of civil war. She worked for China war relief, and founded the East West Association to improve cultural relations and arrange goodwill visits between the United States and Asian nations. After the bombing of Pearl Harbor on December 7, 1941, she tried to stem the anti-Japanese sentiment that many Americans enthusiastically indulged in. Despite all this activity, she made herself write 2,500 words, or ten double-spaced typescript pages,

Here Buck poses with some Asian-American children placed with American families through Welcome House, an adoption agency she founded. Before Welcome House, American adoption agencies refused to place such children in American homes. Buck's foundation helps place thousands of these children in American homes each year.
(Library of Congress)

each day, along with raising five children and supervising the running of her farm.

Although Buck was a prolific writer, through the rest of her life her supreme priority became helping orphaned and abandoned children, of whom there were hundreds of thousands, if not millions, in the wake of World War II. She adopted a total of nine children, many of them of mixed race, and worked to place more such mixed-race children in American homes—a practice that had previously been forbidden by adoption agencies.

In her writing life she sought to escape what she saw as the stigma of her Chinese identity, and in the years immediately following the war produced three novels under the pen name John Sedges, the most successful of which was *The Townsman*, inspired by the life of a cousin of her husband's who had grown up in the Midwest. A popularly received work released under her own name, *The Pavilion of Women* (1946), was about a traditional Chinese matriarch's conversion to Christianity.

When in 1949 the Communist People's Republic of China was established, Buck urged U.S. leaders to continue diplomatic relations with the unorthodox regime, fearing that otherwise the new nation would ally with Russia against America. Her efforts caused her to be blacklisted by Senator Joseph McCarthy, whose witch-hunts targeting suspected Communist sympathizers destroyed many careers. Although Buck was always an outspoken anticommunist, she, too, was temporarily tainted by the Red Scare of the 1950s.

Buck refused to dwell on attacks; she was too busy doing good. In 1949, she had taken the brave step of publishing an article in *The Ladies' Home Journal* entitled "The Child Who Never Grew"—a heartbreaking revelation about her daughter Carol, whose existence few of her public knew about. Again, Buck touched a chord with mass audiences, and thousands of parents of mentally retarded children wrote back to her, thanking her for coming forth with her own story and thereby relieving their own shame and suffering. The next year, the article was expanded into a book of the same name.

It was also at around this time that Buck founded Welcome House, an adoption agency headquartered in a cottage near her Pennsylvania home. The organization was specifically created to place children of mixed American and Asian blood.

In 1953, Buck bought a plot of land in Vermont, where she brought her family each year for camping. There she wrote her autobiography, *My Several Worlds*, published in 1953. That same year, she and Walsh took several of their children on a cross-country automobile trip. In Wyoming, Walsh suffered what was at first diagnosed as a minor heat stroke. But his condition steadily deteriorated, and through the rest of the 1950s, Buck gradually lost her boon companion, editor, and support in life, and came to feel alone in the world long before Walsh's eventual death in 1960. Through these years she continued her active schedule, caring for her family, publishing a stream of critically ignored but best-selling novels, and traveling to Japan for the filming of the movie version of *The Big Wave*. It was there that she was informed of her husband's death. Her desolate feelings at this time were set down in her memoir, *A Bridge for Passing*, published in 1962:

> *Silence, silence everywhere and only silence. I walked beside the sea, so calm that there were no waves, only the swell of the deep tides. I remember how beautiful the landscape was by night . . . I saw everything and felt nothing. It was as though I were floating and far away, in a strange country in which I had no life. I might have been dead myself, so profound was the silence within.*

Though she was nearing seventy, Walsh's death marked a new and active phase of Buck's life. She developed a close friendship, bordering on romance, with Ted Danielewski, the young director who had brought *The Big Wave* and another book, *The Guide*, to the screen. She was a habitué of President John F. Kennedy's White House, where the young leader sought her informal advice on Far Eastern foreign policy. In 1966 she established the Pearl S. Buck Foundation, whose aim was to help Amerasian children overseas who had been fathered and abandoned by American servicemen. She wrote several more books, including novels populated by historical and modern characters of both Far Eastern and American nationality. She also wrote Chinese cookbooks and a chronicle of the Kennedy women. Critics laughed at such novels as *Command the Morning*, a melodrama set in a milieu of rocket scientists and Cold War intrigue, yet many of her works were Book-of-the-Month Club selections, or were excerpted in *Reader's Digest*.

Buck's final project was the revival of a depressed Vermont town, Danby, which she transformed into a historical tourist attraction, providing employment for local residents. She bought a house there, where she lived out her final years. Only in 1972, when she had passed her eightieth birthday, did her health begin to fail. She died peacefully on March 6, 1973, surrounded by her children, and was buried near her Green Hills, Pennsylvania, farmhouse, now the headquarters of the Pearl S. Buck Foundation.

Pearl Buck is remembered more for bringing Chinese culture to the attention of the Western world, and for her many humanitarian achievements, than for the literary merit of her nearly 100 books. She wrote quickly, seldom revising, and her husband's publishing firm—which brought out most of her books until the end of her life—hardly ever edited her work either.

Pearl Buck introduced a broad reading public to the rich and fascinating culture, majestic history, and ongoing human sorrows of what was considered, in the early part of this century, a strange and unknown country. While far from condoning all of China's practices—particularly its unequal treatment of women—she tried to teach Americans to respect other traditions and points of view. Contemporary Chinese-American writers like Amy Tan and Maxine Hong Kingston have explored this culture in more depth, adding their own authentic voices and perspective. It is a development Buck would have applauded.

Buck preached racial and sexual equality long before it was fashionable to do so, almost single-handedly removed the stigma from mixed-race children, and was the first public figure to attempt to lift the veil of shame surrounding mental retardation. Since her death, Buck's humanitarian efforts have continued to bear fruit. Following the fall of Saigon in 1975, the Pearl S. Buck Foundation's "Operation Babylift" brought hundreds of Amerasian infants from Viet Nam to adoptive U.S. homes. Now merged with Welcome House, the foundation is run by Buck's oldest adopted daughter, Janice.

Pearl Buck's life philosophy can best be summed up in a statement she wrote to one of her daughters, who was struggling to become a concert pianist: "The uncommitted life is not worth living; we either believe in something, or we don't." Pearl Buck believed in quite a lot, and managed to enlighten a good portion of the world to what she knew.

Chronology

June 26, 1892	born in Hillsboro, West Virginia; at three months moves to China with family
1911–14	travels to United States to attend Randolph-Macon College in Virginia
1917	marries Lossing Buck in Nanking, China
1918	gives birth to only natural child, Carol Buck
1930	first novel, *East Wind, West Wind*, published by John Day Company
1931	*The Good Earth* published to rave reviews, becomes best-seller
1932	wins Pulitzer Prize in fiction
1936	divorces Lossing Buck; marries her publisher, Richard Walsh; elected member of the National Institute of Arts and Letters
1938	awarded the Nobel Prize in literature
1943	founds Welcome House, adoption agency for mixed-race children
1953	publishes autobiography, *My Several Worlds: A Personal Record*
1961	publishes memoir, *A Bridge for Passing*
1966	establishes Pearl S. Buck Foundation for Amerasian Children
March 6, 1973	dies in Danby, Vermont

Further Reading

Buck's Works

The Good Earth. New York: John Day, 1931. The epic rags-to-riches story that brought the author international renown and the Pulitzer and Nobel prizes.

My Several Worlds: A Personal Record. New York: John Day, 1953. The author's personal memoir of her unusual life as an American citizen whose first home was China.

Books About Buck

La Farge, Ann. *Pearl Buck*. New York: Chelsea House, 1988. Young people's biography with an emphasis on the author's humanitarian work.

Stirling, Nora. *Pearl S. Buck: A Woman in Conflict*. Piscataway, N.J.: New Century Publishers, 1983. Thorough and highly readable biography with a focus on the contradictions within the author's life and work.

Eudora Welty
Capturing the Still Moment

*Eudora Welty brought the South vividly to
life in the stories and novels she wrote
from her home in Jackson, Mississippi.
A pioneer in the Southern Gothic school of
literature, Welty is known for both her
humor and her lushly detailed prose.*
(Library of Congress)

A young woman leaves the safe enclave of her close-knit family
in Jackson, Mississippi and travels south, penetrating the impoverished backwoods corners of her home state, camera in
hand, during the bleakest period of the Depression. The people
living in these furthest outposts of civilization seldom have
basic amenities like indoor plumbing and electricity, and most

125

can't read. But the young journalist is intrigued by the weather-beaten faces of these stoic rural souls, and tries to capture their noble characters in photographic portraits.

At the same time that she is sealing a moment in history on film, the young woman is developing the acute observational skills, the ability to sense and communicate a story, that will serve her so well in her later fiction writing.

Observing and interviewing the rural poor in her job with the Works Progress Administration earned Eudora Welty the intimacy that later helped her to bring these people vividly to life in print. It was here that the author developed the deep sense of place that would serve as the backbone for all her work; in her stories and novels, environments are more than settings; they seem to carry the characters' histories in their very atmosphere. Though she traveled north for her education and to Europe after World War II, throughout her long life Welty has remained based in the South, and it was nearly always of the South that she wrote. Her body of work chronicles the region from its Civil War aftermath through the turmoil of the civil rights movement and on to its current rebirth and modernization.

Welty's stories and novels celebrate the South's myths and traditions, highlighting women's central role in the region's all-important family and community structures. From the illiterate and powerless poor to the eccentric and genteel upper classes, Welty's fiction depicts a wide range of characters who, in the course of grappling with moral questions, help bring the reader to greater understanding of the common human experience.

―――――――

Eudora Alice Welty was born in 1909 in Jackson, Mississippi, the eldest child of Chestina Andrews and Christian Welty. Her father, originally from Ohio, met her mother while briefly working in her native West Virginia, where she was employed as a schoolteacher. The two came to Jackson just after their marriage, and Christian began his successful career at the

Lamar Life Insurance Company, where he eventually rose to the rank of vice president. Because their first child had died shortly after birth, both of Welty's parents were highly protective of Eudora and her two younger brothers. They were great lovers of literature, and made books a priority in their children's lives as well. So great was Mrs. Welty's love of literature that she once ran back into a burning house to save her full set of the works of Charles Dickens.

The Weltys lived in the heart of Jackson, just across the street from Eudora's grammar school, Jefferson Davis Elementary, and a few blocks away from the state capitol building. Her family's interaction with the close-knit social scene of Jackson played a strong part in the fictional technique Welty would eventually master. She would later write in her autobiographical memoirs, *One Writer's Beginnings*, "In Jackson, everything happened in scenes . . . the scene was full of hints, pointers, suggestions and promises of things to find out and know about human beings." Her eccentric neighbors were early sources, both of stories, and of ways in which stories could be told; the long-winded monologues of a talkative neighbor would later supply the format for such stories as "Why I Live at the P.O." The passionate oratory of the traveling evangelists who then roamed the South, and the silent movies that Welty and all the other children flocked to, also contributed to the dramatic sensibility of the young writer-to-be.

Welty had several strong female role models while growing up. Besides her iron-willed mother, young Welty idolized her grammar school principal and the town librarian, both of whom would later serve as the basis for several of the female characters in her fiction. As a child, she was a fierce observer of everything around her. In one of her early short stories, "A Memory," published in 1937, she might have been writing of herself when she wrote in a character's voice, "To watch everything about me I regarded grimly and possessively as a need." The intensity of Welty's childhood memories, the wonder, curiosity, and sense of newness were later captured in such stories as "The Wind," published in her first story collection in 1941.

Childhood trips to her parents' kin in West Virginia and Ohio introduced her to the wider world, and spurred her interest in individual and family histories. She saw the trips themselves as precursors to writing. She wrote of them, "The trips were whole unto themselves. They were stories. Not only in form but in their taking on direction, movement, development, change . . . each trip made its particular revelation . . . When I did begin to write, the short story was a shape that had already formed itself and stood waiting in the back of my mind."

The Welty family was unusually close, happy, and well adjusted, and from the start it supported Eudora's wish to pursue a writing career. Welty would later cite her own independence as a young woman as partly a reaction to her mother's self-sacrificing nature, and partly an emulation of her pioneer grandparents' spirit. Young Welty longed to travel north to attend college, but at sixteen, her parents thought her too young. So in 1925 she set off for Mississippi State College for women, just 200 miles north, in Columbus. Here she quickly established herself as a literary light, writing for the college paper, *The Spectator*, specializing in witty parody pieces. She also sharpened her powers of observation in her study of painting and photography.

After two years, Welty's parents deemed it safe to send her further afield; her father helped her select the University of Wisconsin on the grounds that Wisconsin was a liberal and freethinking state. The dramatic change of environment came as a shock to the young southerner, after the friendly intimacy of the South. The students in Wisconsin seemed, she later wrote, "like sticks of flint that live in the icy world." She would later write of her northern college years, "I used to be in a kind of wandering daze . . . I could feel such a heavy heart inside me . . . it was some kind of desire to be shown that the human spirit was not like that shivering winter in Wisconsin, that the opposite to all this existed in full."

She found spiritual succor in the works of the mystical poets William Butler Yeats and A.E.—the pen name of George William Russell. Their work pointed her in the artistic direction she would eventually pursue.

Though Welty's mother supported her in her wish to become a writer, her father felt that she should also equip herself with the practical skills needed to earn a living. To this end, Welty next traveled to New York City to study business and advertising at the Columbia Graduate School of Business Administration. She found the courses very easy, leaving her enough time to delve into the cultural life of what felt to her like "the center of the world." Her idyll was cut short in 1931, when she was called home because of her father's untimely death from leukemia in 1931, at age fifty-two.

From 1931 through 1933, Welty helped to support her family by working at a series of jobs, one of the first of which was writing the schedule for a radio station housed in the Lamar Life building. After some freelance newspaper writing for local papers, she began her first full-time job with the state office of the Works Progress Administration, where she worked from 1933 through 1936.

As a WPA publicity agent, Welty was assigned to tour the state, taking photographs and writing newspaper stories about the administration's public works projects, which improved living conditions and provided jobs for the rural poor. Welty was deeply struck by what she saw in the course of her work. Then, as now, Mississippi was the poorest state in the nation; illiteracy was common and living was hard in many of the communities she visited. She observed firsthand a country still badly scarred by the Civil War, and a people whose hardships were further compounded by the Depression.

Inspired by the work of photojournalist Margaret Bourke-White, she began taking photographs for her own purposes—mainly stark portraits of the poor people, both black and white, she met in her travels. Eventually shooting over a thousand photographs, she learned that "a good shot doesn't wait." The short-story technique she would later develop, in which a sudden psychological revelation took the place of a traditional plot-driven climax, was partially gleaned from this early photographic experience. Welty wrote essays to accompany her photographs, and during the trips she made to New York whenever her budget allowed, she visited several publishers in the hope of selling them together as a book. Though many publishers expressed interest and admiration for her photographs, several decades would pass before they would find their way into print.

During rest-stops at home, Welty began to write fiction in earnest. Her first efforts narrated the exploits of jaded characters speaking in stilted dialogue, and were set in glamorous but unfamiliar locations such as Paris. Fortunately, Welty had the innate critical sense to realize early that she was pursuing the wrong route, and quickly learned to bring her direct impressions from life to the page. Her first published short story, "Death of a Traveling Salesman," arose from what she had observed of life on the road. The story depicts the inner poverty and spiritual isolation of its title character, which is contrasted with the earthy simplicity of a backwoods family he has stumbled across during his travels.

Welty's career was launched in June 1936, when she was twenty-seven, with the publication of this story in *Manuscript*, a small but important literary magazine. The journal accepted a second story, "Magic," which depicted a bleak sexual encounter between two poor whites, for publication in a later issue the same year. The editor, John Rood, declared that Welty's work was the most exciting American prose he had come across to date. Other acceptances by small literary journals followed, and the larger and more influential *Southern Review* published six of her stories by 1939.

Welty's stories, with their intensely detailed evocations of southern settings and people, and their modernist preoccupation with the psychological drama of the inner life, had begun to garner serious attention in the literary world. Her work caught the eye of the esteemed British writer Ford Madox Ford, but he died before he could bring any of the stories she'd sent him to the attention of a London publisher. Critical to Welty's career development was the support that came from fellow southern writers Katherine Anne Porter and Robert Penn Warren, as well as from Porter's husband, Albert Erskine, all of whom were associated with *The Southern Review*.

An even greater boost to her career came when Doubleday, Doran editor John Woodburn "discovered" her on a scouting trip to the South in 1939. The editor visited the Welty home and returned to New York with a group of her stories, but at first he was unable to persuade his firm to publish them. Short-story collections were harder to publish than novels, and Woodburn felt that the young author needed to create a "buzz" about herself by having her work appear in glossy commercial magazines. To achieve this, she would need the help of an agent. Woodburn gave Welty's stories to Diarmuid Russell, and one of the century's great literary partnerships was born. Russell was the son of the poet A.E., who had been Welty's idol in her student days, and he in turn had a deep appreciation for the young writer's work, which, like his father's, often viewed the world through a mystical lens. Welty's agent would become a lifelong friend as well as literary adviser.

At this time, Welty was living with her mother in Jackson. She spent most of her time writing fiction, with occasional forays into journalism to make ends meet. The South at this time was undergoing a literary renaissance, led by William Faulkner, who lived down the road in Oxford; other important figures included Welty's new supporters Warren and Porter. Welty's social and literary life was centered around a group of southern literary enthusiasts, both readers and aspiring writers. This group of mostly young men met frequently for dinner and discussion in each other's homes. Through this group Welty met John Robinson, who would be her friend and lover through the war years and beyond.

By 1940, Russell had succeeded in placing two of Welty's stories in key commercial magazines—one in the *Atlantic Monthly*, and one in *Harper's*. In addition, Welty was awarded prestigious fellowships. The first sent her to the Breadloaf

Writers' Conference in 1940, the second to the Yaddo writers' colony the following year. The editors at Doubleday were ready to put out Welty's first collection.

The stories in *A Curtain of Green*, published in 1941, were among the first to embody not only Welty's, but an entire school of southern writing. The eccentric, psychotic, and maimed individuals populating many of these tales would become emblematic of a style of writing that came to be known as "Southern Gothic," and would later be embraced by such writers as Carson McCullers and Flannery O'Connor. While some critics called such characters needlessly grotesque, Katherine Anne Porter, in her glowing introduction to Welty's first book, defended them as "individuals exactly and clearly presented."

The title story is about a woman whose husband was killed when a tree fell on him in their own backyard. Rather than trying to control the vegetation that took her mate, the half-mad woman seeks to become part of it, spending her days in her backyard, nurturing its untamed growth. The most anthologized Welty story, "Why I Live at the P.O." also comes from this first collection. A comic first-person monologue of an eccentric, this story showcased the young author's perfect ear for dialogue as it detailed the mean-spirited interactions of a disturbed southern family. As with many of the other stories in this collection, its theme is one of spiritual isolation. While Welty's reputation among serious literary writers grew with the publication of her first collection, reviews among northern critics were mixed.

Welty's first novel, *The Robber Bridegroom*, emerged from a story originally submitted for this collection, which on the advice of her agent was expanded into a short book that was published in 1942. Set in the antebellum South and drawing heavily from fairy tales, myths, and American folklore, *The Robber Bridegroom* explores the duality of human nature—the title character is both the villain and hero. The novel is also part of the southern oral storytelling tradition, full of puns and humorous asides. While many critics conceded the book's entertainment value, praise by the mass media was again limited.

But Welty's star was on an irreversible upswing; in 1941, she won the first of many O. Henry awards, the second-place prize, for "A Worn Path," published in the *Atlantic Monthly*. In 1942 she was awarded her first Guggenheim fellowship, as well as the first of two back-to-back first-place O. Henry prizes—the first for the title story of her second collection, *The Wide Net*, and the second for "Livvie Is Back" in 1943.

During World War II, Welty was asked by the State Department to do war publicity, but the idea of popularizing violence was repellent to her, and she declined the offer. Around this time Welty often complained of suffering from writer's block because of worry about her two brothers and her friend John Robinson, who were all fighting in Europe, but she managed to produce enough stories to fill a fine second collection, *The Wide Net*, which was published in 1943. The stories in Welty's new book were well removed from the horrors of modern times. All were set in the vicinity of the Natchez Trace, a road leading north from Jackson, Mississippi, but they differed in subject, period, and characterization. In common, they were all weakly plotted and were concerned instead with the characters' inner lives. They demanded, according to Welty biographer Michael Kreyling, "a new logic that Welty herself only barely knew"—one that used juxtaposition, symbolism, and close attention to the nuances of the heart, rather than the logic of an action-driven plot. It was almost as if the author were searching for an alternative interpretation of the human experience, one that stressed the internal struggles of the individual rather than the external violence of the war.

In the title story, a backwoods rural community drags a river for the body of a young pregnant bride, who has left a note threatening to drown herself after her husband stayed out all night. The journey becomes an important ritual for all who take part in it, yet for the wayward bride, the real motivation is that "she had been filled to the brim with that elation that they all remembered . . . the elation that comes of great hopes and changes . . ." An old-timer who has supplied the net for the expedition seems to know that there will be no bride retrieved from the watery depths, yet he understands that the search itself is serving an important psychological function for all of its participants. "A Still Moment" brings together in one story the historical figures Lorenzo Dow, a famous evangelist; John James Audubon, the painter and naturalist; and James Murrell, the legendary murderer. The three men meet by accident on the Natchez Trace and experience a moment of transcendent recognition when each is enraptured by the sight of a pure white heron. Another story, "On the Landing," is a tour de force in which a young woman escapes from the control of her grandfather only to fall in thrall to a wandering, indifferent lover. This story is striking for its contrasts between the lyrical language in which the girl's ecstatic feelings of love are described and the shocking depiction of primitive backwoods male sexuality.

When *The Wide Net* was published, Welty's dreamy, richly textured prose was attacked by some critics as doing little more than create a mood. But the author had a staunch defender in one editor, *Harper's Bazaar*'s Mary Louise Aswell, who cherished her stories' crucial "moment of recognition" that captured a change in human consciousness.

Welty spent part of the war years in New York City, writing book reviews for *The New York Times*, marking the beginning of a long career in literary criticism that would provide financial sustenance throughout her life. In 1944 the author's status was further bolstered by a grant from the American Academy of Arts and Letters. Though her literary career was flourishing, Welty continued to worry about her two brothers fighting overseas, as well as about her friend John Robinson. To cheer Robinson up, she sent him installations of her work-in-progress, which would be published as a book, *Delta Wedding*, in 1946. In fact, Robinson, a member of an old Mississippi family that had lived in the Delta since antebellum times, was the source of much of the material in her second novel. A frequent visitor to his ancestral home during his absence, Welty even perused the personal diary of one of his female antecedents for material. Welty found the rich family life documented there both restricting and rewarding; she would explore family themes, using this material again in a later story called "Kin."

Delta Wedding appeared first in serialized form in *The Atlantic Monthly*, and was published by Harcourt, Brace, where she had followed her Doubleday editor, Edward Weeks. When her new novel came out, many northern critics called it a southern fantasy, accusing the author of whitewashing the South's dark past. Welty complained to her friend and agent Russell that "the North simply does not comprehend the South and for that reason will always cherish a kind of fury at it, it doesn't understand our delights and pleasures or even anything abstract about our ways." A *New York Times* critic was slightly more generous, commenting accurately that "the light comes obliquely in Welty's writing." The author was finally vindicated by the unrestrained praise of the influential critic Edmund Wilson, who until then had been notorious for his scorn of southern writers.

At the war's end, Welty was overjoyed to have both her brothers and Robinson return unscathed. She spent the years 1946 through 1950 happily wandering—she made two long trips to San Francisco, part of the time living with Robinson, and also enjoyed a long stay in New York. During these traveling years she worked on a group of stories that would form a coherent work—more like a novel than a story collection. The result, *The Golden Apples*, was eventually published in 1949. While on the West Coast, Welty lectured on writing at the Northwest Pacific Writers' Conference held at Seattle's University of Washington. In the summer of 1948 she lived happily in New York, collaborating on a humorous musical review called "Bye Bye Brevoort," which was never produced. Welty hardly minded; she was glad to have an excuse to be in the city and attend the theater at least once a week.

As she completed the stories that would become *The Golden Apples*, each was accepted by a major literary review, but each was met with puzzlement, for the individual stories failed to make their full impact standing alone. The author ruminated to Russell that "the ash can" might be the best destiny for the stories in this innovative and risk-taking collection; she herself hardly understood them as they issued from her typewriter. While each story suffered from the by-now common criticism of weak plotting, Welty slowly began to see the collection as giving a distanced overview of a community advancing through time, zeroing in now on one character, now on another.

One writer and critic who did appreciate Welty's approach was the Irish writer Elizabeth Bowen, who herself also used an oblique or veiled storytelling method. When *The Golden Apples*, probably Welty's finest literary achievement, was finally published as a collection in 1949, its coherence was made clear, and Bowen was joined in her praise by almost universally positive notices.

The stories each focus on a different drama at a different period in the life of a character in the small Deep South community of Morgana. The book is heavy with references to Greek mythology, with the wandering, sexually potent, mysterious and much-feared King McClain standing in for the Greek God Zeus. One long story, "June Recital," follows the decline of a German immigrant piano teacher, a stranger to this close-knit community, and her wayward star pupil, Virgie Rainey, the heroine of the entire collection. The story explores the failed relationship between the two women and draws its poignancy from the characters' inability to help each other. The final story, "The Wanderers," is Virgie Rainey's story—an articulation of her place and conception of community and a celebration of the glorious duality of life:

> *Virgie never saw it differently, never doubted that all the opposites on earth were close together, love close to hate, living to dying; but of them all, hope and despair were the closest blood—unrecognizable one from the other sometimes, making moments double upon themselves, and in the doubling double again, amending but never taking back.*

The intertwined structure of *The Golden Apples* demonstrates Welty's philosophy of writing as explained in her memoirs: "It is our inward journey that leads us through time—forward or back, seldom in a straight line, most often spiralling. Each of us is moving, changing, with respect to others. As we discover, we remember, remembering, we discover, and most intensely do we experience this when our separate journeys converge. Our living experience at those meeting points is one of the charged dramatic fields of fiction."

While the book was at press, Welty learned that she'd won another Guggenheim. Now she was routinely being referred to, in the literary press, as a "master." In the early 1950s the author used her Guggenheim money to travel to Europe, where she lectured at Cambridge University on "Place in Fiction." She also met Elizabeth Bowen; the two would remain lifelong friends and would often host each other in their respective homes in Ireland and in Jackson.

In 1951, Welty was elected to the National Institute of Arts and Letters, and again settled down in Mississippi, where she remained for a few years, except for a few trips to New York. Though she and Robinson were assumed by many friends to be close to marriage at this time, a permanent union was never forged, though the two remained lifelong friends. Robinson himself pursued a marginal, wandering writer's life, never achieving the literary acclaim of his famous friend.

In 1954 Welty published the book *The Ponder Heart*, a comic novel, which won the author the William Dean Howells Medal from the Academy of Arts and Letters, and which would also enjoy a long second life in the theater. The stories that were collected in *The Bride of the Inisfallen*, published in 1955, though previously published in top-paying journals, were of lesser quality than those in her previous collection. They tended toward excessive diffuseness; their themes were often mysterious, though their moods and details were, as always, strong. Welty used as her settings variously the contemporary South, the Civil War South, and the postwar Europe of her recent travels. One story from this collection, "The Burning,"

Eudora Welty, second from right, with cast members of The Ponder Heart,
*a theatrical adaptation of her comic novel of the same name, which was
produced as a Broadway play in 1956.*
(Library of Congress)

about two southern belles facing the marauding soldiers of
Sherman's march, won her another O. Henry award in 1951.

In 1955, Welty again traveled overseas, lecturing at Cambridge University in England and visiting Elizabeth Bowen
at her estate in Ireland, but the mid-1950s brought an unexpected stall in her literary career. The author's attention and
energy were increasingly diverted to caring for her mother,
who was suffering from eye problems, and her two younger
brothers, who suffered from arthritis. Always unusually devoted to her family, Welty was desolate when her brother
Walter died suddenly in 1959, at age forty-three. The only
fiction she published for several years was *The Shoe Bird*, a
children's book, in 1964. Journalism and several books of
literary commentary, as well as a brief teaching stint at

Jackson's Millsaps College, helped to defray her mother's nursing home expenses.

While her family responsibilities took a clear priority over her fictional output during these difficult years, she was very much aware of the drastically changing times. On learning of the assassination of civil rights leader Medgar Evers, right in her own town of Jackson, Mississippi, in June of 1963, Welty sat down and wrote, "Where Is the Voice Coming From?" in one sitting the very night the murder occurred. The story is the first-person narrative of the white murderer whose perceived racial superiority is threatened by all that Evers represents:

> There was one way left, for me to be ahead of you and stay ahead of you . . . Now I'm alive and you ain't. We ain't never now going to be equals and you know why? One of us is dead.

Of the event and the story it prompted, Welty explained, "Whoever the murderer is, I know him: not his identity, but his coming about, in this time and place." The story was quickly published in *The New Yorker*. Another story, "The Demonstrators," published in 1966, was a portrait of the private tragedy of a sorrowful white man set against the backdrop of the larger tragedy of the violence and seething suspicion that characterized Mississippi during the civil rights years.

In 1966, Welty's mother died, and her other brother succumbed suddenly just four days later. Saddened and drained, Welty turned her attention to completing the novel she had been working on sporadically for ten years. *Losing Battles*, a tragicomic southern novel of eccentric character and plotting, was set in the backwoods Mississippi of the 1930s. Like her earlier novels, it studied family life and commented on the duality of human nature; unlike them, it was fast-moving, and made greater use of dialogue and plot.

The novel was poorly received by Harcourt Brace when she submitted it in 1969; in the realistic-minded 1960s, the editors at Harcourt were looking for work that confronted the current racial inequities in the South, and Welty's work didn't fill the bill. The book's treatment eventually caused her to break with her publisher, and her agent Diarmuid Russell sold the novel to Random House, where it was edited by her old associate from *The Southern Review*, Albert Erskine. In his hands, the book was well handled and well promoted when published in 1970, and quickly found a place high on the best-seller list—the first of her books to do so. Random House was also quick to recognize an item in her unpublished repertoire that *did* comment on relevant social issues: The next year, the publisher brought out her backwoods Depression photographs under the title *One Time, One Place: Mississippi in the Depression; A Snapshot Album*.

Welty's comeback was crowned in 1972 with the publication and surprise commercial success of her short novel *The Optimist's Daughter*, which had first appeared in *The New Yorker* in 1969. Set in the contemporary South, it is the story of a young widow's contemplation of her father—a retired judge based on the author's own father. Unlike the father, the heroine, Laurel, is not an optimist, and returns to her home in Chicago from her visit south with a sense of emptiness and disappointment over a lost world. The novel, in addition to reaching the top of the best-seller list, added to Welty's long list of prizes, winning the gold medal for fiction from the American Academy of Arts and Letters and the Pulitzer, in 1973.

Completely unexpectedly, the book made Welty a living legend, and ushered in the "Leading Woman of Letters" status that remains hers today. On May 2, 1973, she presided over the first annual "Eudora Welty Day" in Jackson, and innumerable honorary degrees and merits of recognition have followed. Welty has taught periodically at Oxford and Cambridge Universities, and was recognized with awards by Presidents Jimmy Carter and Ronald Reagan. In 1978, a collection of her nonfiction prose was published as *The Eye of the Story*, and in 1980 *The Collected Stories of Eudora Welty* brought all her short fiction together in one volume. *One*

Writer'sBeginnings, her autobiographical memoirs, itself became a best-seller when published in 1984.

━━━━━━━━━━

Eudora Welty still lives in the house where she was born, the undisputed favorite citizen of Jackson. She guards her privacy closely, preferring to live not as the famous writer but as a member of the community. Physical ailments have largely put a halt to her writing, but she grants occasional interviews to the press and lends her support on behalf of writers' freedom around the world to the writers' organization, PEN.

Though her overall output is rather small—fewer than half of her twenty-seven books are works of fiction—Welty's literary reputation is gargantuan; many critics consider her the finest short-story writer America has produced in this century. She is considered influential in the development of the "Southern Renaissance" of the mid-twentieth century, paving the way for Carson McCullers and Flannery O'Connor, and is viewed as a literary descendant of Gertrude Stein, James Joyce, and Virginia Woolf.

Her biographer Michael Kreyling has commented, "Welty really invented a new way of telling a story . . . her stories meandered, just as life did, with weird sorts of jumps—all of which, according to the formula, were a violation, but she made it work."

Of her stories, Welty commented in the preface to her collected stories, "If they have any special virtue . . . it would lie in the fact that they are stories written from within. They come from living here—they were *part* of living here, of my loving familiarity with the thoughts and feelings of those around me, in their many shadings and variations and contradictions."

Welty may be indelibly tied in the reading public's mind to one particular place, but her stories are consistently accessible to all.

Chronology

April 13, 1909	born in Jackson, Mississippi
1925–27	attends Mississippi State College for Women
1927–29	earns B.A. degree from University of Wisconsin
1930–31	studies advertising at Columbia University
1931–33	works in newspapers and radio in Jackson
1933–36	travels through Mississippi as WPA publicity agent
1936	first stories, "Death of a Traveling Salesman" and "Magic," published in *Manuscript* to critical acclaim
1941	first story collection, *A Curtain of Green*, published; wins second-place O. Henry award for "A Worn Path"
1942	first novel, *The Robber Bridegroom*, published; wins first-place O. Henry award for "The Wide Net"
1942–43	wins Guggenheim fellowship; wins first-place O. Henry award for "Livvie Is Back"
1944	receives grant from American Academy of Arts and Letters
1949	*The Golden Apples* published; receives renewal of Guggenheim fellowship, travels to Europe
1951	wins first-place O. Henry award for "The Burning"
1955	lectures at Cambridge University in England; awarded William Dean

	Howells Medal of the Academy of Arts and Letters
1972	receives gold medal for fiction from American Academy of Arts and Letters
1973	receives Pulitzer Prize for *The Optimist's Daughter*
1980	receives National Medal of Literature and Medal of Freedom Award

Further Reading

Welty's Works

The Collected Stories of Eudora Welty. New York: Harcourt Brace Jovanovich, 1980.

One Time, One Place: Mississippi in the Depression; A Snapshot Album. New York: Random House, 1971. The author's long unpublished photographic portraits of the rural poor; originally taken during the Depression during her Works Progress Administration stint, finally brought to print more than thirty years later.

One Writer's Beginnings. Cambridge, Mass.: Harvard University Press, 1984. The author's best-selling memoirs of her childhood and the influences that shaped her writing.

The Optimist's Daughter. New York: Random House, 1972. The Pulitzer Prize–winning novel of the contemporary South that brought the author's works to a wide readership.

Books About Welty

Binding, Paul. *The Still Moment: Eudora Welty: Portrait of a Writer*. London: Virago, 1994. Loving and thorough analysis of the writer's life and work.

Kreyling, Michael. *Author and Agent: Eudora Welty & Diarmuid Russell*. New York: Farrar, Straus & Giroux, 1991. Details the warm and productive relationship between the author and her agent; includes much entertaining and revealing correspondence.

Flannery O'Connor: Writer of Violence and Vision

Flannery O'Connor lived most of her abbreviated writing life on her mother's isolated dairy farm in rural Georgia. In her fiction she would use this limited landscape, and the Christian fundamentalists who populated it, to communicate universal themes
(Library of Congress)

*I*t is a hot afternoon in the Deep South. A southern family is traveling to Florida: father, mother, baby, children, and grandmother all jammed together in one car. They are a typical family—the parents tired and preoccupied, the children grousing and moaning, the grandmother inwardly criticizing all of them. The grandmother has secretly smuggled her cat on the

145

trip in a picnic basket. When the cat suddenly jumps out and onto the father's shoulder, he is so startled that he loses control of the vehicle, and the car tumbles down a ravine. While the family members are only slightly injured, their troubles have just begun. They have stumbled into the lair of "The Misfit"—an escaped mass murderer. The Misfit and his companions march each member of the family into the surrounding woods, one by one. The grandmother hears gunshots ring out as each is executed. She is the last to go. She gathers her wits and tries to reason with the Misfit, pleading for her life. "I know you wouldn't shoot a lady!"

In response, the Misfit calmly explains that his rationale for murder is his lack of faith in Jesus. "If He did what He said, then it's nothing for you to do but throw away everything and follow Him, and if He didn't, then it's nothing for you to do but enjoy the few minutes you got left the best way you can—by killing somebody or burning down his house or doing some other meanness to him."

Though overcome with horror, the grandmother tries to connect with the murderer on a human level: "Why you're one of my babies. You're one of my own children!" When she tries to touch him on the shoulder, he shoots her three times in the chest, killing her instantly.

"She would of been a good woman," her executor remarks to an accomplice, "if it had been somebody to shoot her every minute of her life."

The story, "A Good Man Is Hard to Find," is one of Flannery O'Connor's most striking and characteristic works: Ordinary people are thrown into extraordinary circumstances, forcing them to confront questions of faith. O'Connor used violence and grotesque characters modeled on her Georgia neighbors to deliver a religious message to a largely skeptical reading public.

Crippled by chronic illness at twenty-six, O'Connor rarely left her mother's rural Georgia farm during the course of her short but brilliant writing life. Like the poet Emily Dickinson, another great American author who lived a severely restricted life, O'Connor transcended the boundaries of her daily experience with a far-reaching imagination and a masterful ability to relate the local to the cosmic. During her lifetime, her readers recognized her power, but many missed her point. Yet her two novels and twenty stories achieved insights into human fallibility and the meaning of existence that are unparalleled in American literature today.

Mary Flannery O'Connor was born on March 25, 1925 in Savannah, Georgia, the only child of Regina Cline and Edward O'Connor, a businessman who made a comfortable living in real estate. Until the age of twelve, O'Connor lived in the historic and elegant coastal city, which had been the state's original center of learning and culture. The O'Connors lived across the street from St. John the Baptist Cathedral, and Mary Flannery attended Catholic grade school there. As a child, O'Connor would often surprise her father by hiding her own short verse compositions under his napkin at the dinner table. Edward O'Connor was himself a literary man, and he encouraged his only child to appreciate reading and learning. His daughter grew up assured of her own intelligence, talents, and Catholic beliefs, though she would later cheerfully describe her childhood appearance as "pigeon-toed" with "a receding chin."

From childhood, O'Connor was fascinated by birds. At age five she owned a chicken that had the unique ability to walk both forwards and backwards—a feat that brought O'Connor and her pet to the attention of a local news service, which ran a photo story on it. Later O'Connor, in typical humorous fashion, would insist that this event had been the high point in her life; everything that came afterward was an anticlimax. When she became a writer, birds, and particularly the majestic peacock, would serve as important religious symbols in her fiction.

When O'Connor was twelve, her father was stricken with lupus, a rare and disabling immune system disorder that would kill him less than three years later. After the lupus diagnosis, the family moved for his health to her mother's native home town of Milledgeville, an inland city that had been Georgia's capital before the Civil War. Her mother's family, the Clines, were important in the community; her grandfather had served as mayor for twenty-two years, and his mansion had once been the governor's residence. The change of environment was jarring to O'Connor; her family was different from their neighbors, being well-off Catholics in a predominantly poor, Protestant fundamentalist town. More-over, Milledgeville, unlike cosmopolitan Savannah, was steeped in racial prejudice, ignorance, and a longing for the order of pre–Civil War times.

There was no Catholic school in the area, so O'Connor attended Milledgeville's public high school, which she found inferior in the quality and scope of education it provided. Nonetheless, O'Connor began to develop her creative talents and to display the capacity for irreverent humor that would inject such original vitality into her fiction. In a high school home economics class, when instructed to fashion an outer-wear garment for a small child, O'Connor arrived leading a chicken decked out in a piqué coat. She continued to write poetry, studied painting, and demonstrated a distinct talent for cartooning. She would later say that the art of cartooning provided useful lessons for short-story writing; both must use exaggeration and simplification to get a point across quickly and boldly. At this time O'Connor also tested her writing skills by penning a series of books she never attempted to pub-lish—comic sketches of relatives and a personal journal.

O'Connor's father died when she was fifteen, and after gradu-ating from high school, she enrolled in Milledgeville's Georgia State College for Women. Though she had aimed for a career in either fiction writing or cartooning, O'Connor was discour-aged by the indifference of the professors in her college's English department, and she switched her major to social science. But she continued to write for the student paper, to which she contributed a weekly cartoon. During her college years she submitted many cartoons to *The New Yorker*, but none were purchased. She also contributed stories to the campus literary quarterly. At least one professor was perceptive enough to spot her writing talent, and he sent one of her stories to the Writers' Workshop at the University of Iowa. The result was a graduate fellowship at the Writers' Workshop there. Already confident that she was on her way to establishing a literary career, O'Connor legally dropped her first name, Mary, surmising that the bland, parochial sound of her original name would doom any work she published under it to obscurity.

Writers' Workshop director Paul Engle could barely understand a word of O'Connor's Georgia drawl at their first interview; he asked her to write her questions down on a piece of paper. But he was already deeply impressed with the young writer's talent, and would be an important mentor. In graduate school, O'Connor was shy about reading her stories aloud and arranged to have them read anonymously. She rarely participated in the heated class discussions, preferring to sit in the back, smiling wryly when the humorous effects of her stories garnered a response from the class; but she was undoubtedly the most outstanding student.

O'Connor was pleased with the hard-working, literary atmosphere of graduate school, after what she considered a mediocre undergraduate education. It wasn't until she attended Iowa that she was introduced to important modernist writers such as James Joyce and T. S. Eliot, as well as the southern writers Robert Penn Warren and William Faulkner, who, as a visiting professor, critiqued her early work. Through this circle she met the writer Caroline Gordon, a fellow Catholic who also worked with Christian themes and symbols; O'Connor would send Gordon her manuscripts for criticism throughout her life.

O'Connor's first stories began to be accepted for publication while she was still in graduate school. In 1946, *Accent* published her first story, "The Geranium," which was about a racist old man living in physical and spiritual isolation. Like the other five stories that would comprise her master's thesis, it was a bleakly set characterization of a rural Georgian, with a strong religious theme. She began to write her first novel, eventually titled *Wise Blood*, while in graduate school; it won her the Rinehart Iowa Prize for a first novel in 1946, funded by the New York publisher Holt, Rinehart, which planned to publish the work when completed. After being awarded her master's degree in 1947, O'Connor continued on at Iowa for another year, working as a teaching assistant and making progress on her novel. Engle recalled the nascent author at this time as being single-minded in her pursuit of good craftsmanship, always willing to revise her work in response to criticism.

On the basis of her strong start, O'Connor was invited to spend the winter of 1948 at Yaddo, the writers' colony in Saratoga Springs, New York. At Yaddo she met the agent Elizabeth McKee, who placed another story, "The Capture," in *Mademoiselle* that year. Three other stories, all episodes in the novel she was struggling to complete, were soon accepted by the literary journals *Tomorrow* and *The Partisan Review*. At Yaddo, O'Connor also met the poet Robert Lowell, who introduced her to Robert Giroux, of the New York publishing firm Farrar, Straus, Cudahy, which would later publish her work. Lowell also introduced the young writer to Robert and Sally Fitzgerald, intellectuals who would become lifelong friends.

In 1949, O'Connor briefly rented an apartment in New York, but soon forsook city life to live with the Fitzgeralds in rural Ridgefield, Connecticut. Robert Fitzgerald was a poet who taught at Sarah Lawrence College, and Sally raised their three children. O'Connor lived quietly as a paying boarder; all of her life she would best thrive artistically in quiet rural settings.

O'Connor and the Fitzgeralds shared many common religious, philosophical, and literary concerns. After World War II, the pervasive philosophical mood was one of existentialism, which operated on the assumption that nothing existed beyond the present. God was frequently proclaimed to be dead; to many, the looming threat of atomic warfare rendered religion meaningless.

Such theories were a challenge to these young Catholic intellectuals. In her novel in progress, as well as in later-published stories such as "Good Country People," O'Connor would try to demonstrate that the moral structure provided by religion was indispensable in the simplest activities of everyday life.

O'Connor struggled long with her first novel; she knew what she wanted to say, but took many wrong turns before successfully saying it. The book's hero is Hazel Motes, a young man raised as a Christian fundamentalist who loses his faith during the war and returns to find his rural Georgia home and community likewise vanished. A sense of sin is the only remnant of his evangelical religion, and like many O'Connor characters to come, Hazel Motes will eventually find religion only by immersing himself in sin. The novel is populated with the odd, violent, and gruesomely maimed characters that would cause O'Connor's writing to be tagged with the label "Southern Grotesque," a label she deplored. She used these characters and actions for a reason. Explains Robert Fitzgerald, "In 1949–50 . . . the horror of the recent human predicament had not been lost on us. Flannery felt that an artist who was a Catholic should face all the truth down to the worst of it."

Her prospective publisher, Holt, Rinehart, was dismayed at the increasingly sordid installments the author was sending for review; they feared that the book's stark situations and extreme violence would alienate readers. O'Connor disagreed, and was eventually released from her contract. Harcourt, Brace would eventually publish the work in 1952.

O'Connor was traveling home by train for a Christmas visit to her mother in December of 1950 when disaster struck; she came down with the high fevers of the systemic lupus that had killed her father. The young writer's life hung in the balance in an Atlanta hospital for several months before a combination of blood transfusions and drugs controlled the worst effects of the disease, and she went into remission. At the time, lupus had not been known to be hereditary; when O'Connor awoke from a coma, it was with the expectation that she had only a few years left to live.

When in the early summer of 1950 O'Connor was ready to leave the hospital, she was far too weak to live on her own. She and her mother settled at Andalusia, a 150-year-old working dairy farm outside Milledgeville that her mother had inherited from her brother. For the remainder of her life, O'Connor would seldom leave this spot, whose wood-edged red fields and fiery sunsets would serve as the backdrop for so many of her stories.

Regarding her illness, O'Connor always maintained an accepting stance, undoubtedly related to her deep religious beliefs. She felt blessed to be forced into a quiet and isolated life, which was perfectly suited to her vocation, but she was in fact often exhausted by the disease. Lupus produces antibodies that attack the body's own tissues; its side effects include severe arthritis, high fevers, and the disintegration of vital organs such as the kidneys. The disease is controlled only with strong drugs such as cortisone and prednisone, which themselves induce severe and debilitating side effects; in time the drugs weakened O'Connor's bones so that she could walk only with the aid of crutches.

O'Connor kept to a strict and unwavering schedule in the slow completion of her novel. After attending early morning mass, she wrote from nine to twelve in the morning, enjoyed a good lunch with her mother, usually at the Sanford House Hotel in Milledgeville, then spent the afternoon recuperating from her efforts—tending her garden and admiring the peacocks she had begun to keep, if feeling well, quietly reading or resting if not.

Unquestionably, living under the constant threat of death influenced O'Connor's writing; her religious themes are played out, like Greek tragedies, with moral questions framed in life and death situations. She herself attributed her concern with mortality to her Catholicism: "I'm a born Catholic and death has always been brother to my imagination."

O'Connor found her immediate surroundings a rich source; the casts of characters in many of her stories would closely mirror the hierarchy among her neighbors, who consisted of hard-headed farm widows like her mother, white tenant farmers, and black farmhands. One hard-working Polish refugee employed by Regina O'Connor would become the model for Guizac, the Christlike title character in one of her most acclaimed stories, "The Displaced Person."

When O'Connor's first novel, *Wise Blood*, was published in 1952, it was greeted with reviews that ranged from admiring to uncomprehending to outraged. Some critics compared it with the work of existentialist writers Albert Camus and Jean-Paul Sartre. Like those authors, O'Connor depicts an existence empty of meaning and characterized by spiritual alienation. But unlike them, she refers back to religion as an answer.

The hero of her novel, Hazel Motes, returns disillusioned from the war wishing to be converted, and to convert others, to "nothing." He apes the ubiquitous southern evangelists, but is promoting what he calls "The Church Without Jesus Christ." As in many works of fiction to come, the author will attempt to show that the choice is not between God and nothing, but God and evil; the devil's greatest trick is "convincing us he doesn't exist," the author would later surmise.

After spending the book denying Christ, Motes commits a senseless murder, after which he blinds himself, then suffers a Christlike death. The book is laden with symbolism; the title character's name indicates that a "haze" obscures his spiritual vision, that he has a "mote" in the eye. The "wise blood" of the title alludes to Christ's blood; though shed through violence, it eventually redeems. Throughout, the harshness of the novel is relieved by deadpan humor. Explanations like "It was plain that she was so well adjusted she didn't have to think anymore" poke fun at the complacency of nonbelievers.

O'Connor's social life during these years was restricted to her mother and an uncle, who also lived on the farm, and a small group of literary neighbors, who met to read and critique each other's work. Because she chose to address her religious themes via characters who were Christian fundamentalists, rather than Catholics, O'Connor was viewed somewhat suspiciously by some of her neighbors, who, mis-understanding her work, felt that she was making fun of them. Though O'Connor leavened her stories with strong doses of humor that exposed the pride and foibles of her characters, she used her own immediate surroundings as the setting for her stories because they were uniquely suited for playing out her religious themes. In contrast to most of the rest of the country, in the southern "Bible belt" religion was still very much a part of people's everyday lives and provided O'Connor's characters with a believable language of symbols and allegory. Moreover, the South, she felt, was an especially suitable setting for her tales of redemption, having itself, like the Garden of Eden, experienced a "fall"—its defeat in the Civil War after the moral quagmire of slavery.

As her stories began to be published in prestigious literary journals, O'Connor was recognized with awards—she received fellowships from the *Kenyon Review*, which published many of her stories, in 1953 and 1954. In 1955, Harcourt, Brace published her first short-story collection, *A Good Man Is Hard to Find*. The violence of the title story, about the abduction and murder of a Georgia family, seemed sensational to many readers. This was frustrating to O'Connor, who would later explain, "in my own stories . . . violence is strangely capable of returning my characters to reality and preparing them to accept their moment of grace. Their heads are so hard that almost nothing else will do the work."

The author's favorite of the ten stories was "The Artificial Nigger," which follows a day-visit to Atlanta by two backwoods Georgians, a righteous old grandfather and his grandson, Nelson. The two are disoriented by the large, threatening city, and when Nelson accidentally knocks down a woman, the grandfather, Mr. Head, denies association with him—an allusion to Peter's denial of Christ. The two are reconciled in a transcendent moment when, wandering lost and estranged, they come across a small plaster statue of a black man decorating a genteel front lawn. Both Nelson and his grandfather are awestruck; the figure acts as a conduit for God's grace, inducing the grandfather to repent and acknowledge his faults. At the story's end the two characters are united in love and humility.

In another story, "Good Country People," the emptiness of the atheism professed by the proud young woman who has changed her name from Joy to Hulga is symbolized by her artificial leg. The thirty-two-year-old Ph.D., who thinks herself above her simple-minded mother and neighbors, sets out to seduce a seemingly innocent traveling Bible salesman who describes himself as "just a country boy." After stealing her false leg, the young man reveals his true, malevolent nature, telling Joy-Hulga, "You ain't so smart . . . I been believing in nothing ever since I was born!"

In "The Displaced Person," an industrious Polish Catholic named Guizac threatens the order of the farm where he has found refuge after the war, first through his hard work, which shows up the laziness of the other farm workers, then by trying to arrange a green-card marriage between his young cousin, still trapped in a European refugee camp, and one of the black farmhands. The farm's owner, tenants, and farmhands all collude in the displaced Guizac's only semi-accidental death. In the story, a peacock is a central symbol of Christ. The visiting priest who has placed Guizac on the farm remarks on viewing the peacock's rare, full-feathered display, "Christ will come like that!"

In the latter 1950s O'Connor wrote steadily, and her literary reputation continued to grow; she was honored with a grant from the National Institute of Arts and Letters in 1957, and received a Ford Foundation grant in 1959 to complete another novel in progress. During these years she felt well enough to accept invitations to lecture at colleges and universities, where she took the opportunity to explain her religious and literary philosophy. In one of these lectures, she equated the writer's job with that of a religious prophet; it was the job of each to see through reality, as well as call attention to forgotten truths. Though O'Connor herself had studied in a writing program, she had little praise for such programs in general. To be a good writer, she told one audience of aspirants, one needed "vision . . . and you do not get this from a writing class."

In 1958 O'Connor traveled with her mother and a cousin to Lourdes, the holy site in France where the Virgin Mary was reputed to have appeared and cured the sick, and to Rome, where she had an audience with the pope. According to her friend Robert Fitzgerald, with whom she kept up a steady correspondence, she made the pilgrimage only for the sake of her mother and cousin, and actually dreaded the possibility of a miracle cure. She had always accepted, even welcomed her disease as a blessing both to her art and to her spiritual development. On her return she quipped to her friend Fitzgerald in a letter, "I had the best looking crutches in Europe."

Because the editors she had been working with at Harcourt, Brace had left the company, O'Connor sought to be released from her contract with the firm. Her next novel would be published by Farrar, Straus, Cudahy, under the guidance of her friend Robert Giroux, who had been a supporter and literary confidant since their meeting at Yaddo in 1948.

Many critics consider O'Connor's second novel, *The Violent Bear It Away*, to be her best work. Like her first novel, it is the story of a young man who tries to reject his religious destiny. Fourteen-year-old Francis Tarwater has been raised by an evangelical grandfather and told that his destiny is to preach and baptize—specifically, to baptize his six-year-old cousin, Bishop. Bishop is the son of Rayber, a schoolteacher who has rejected his evangelical heritage and hopes to persuade his nephew, Tarwater, to do the same. The book is Tarwater's struggle between his religious destiny and the devil, who comes first in the form of a voice, then embodied in an actual person. Enlightenment comes to Tarwater only after the drowning of his cousin during the bungled baptism and a rape by a drifter who is the physical embodiment of the devil. The book is tightly structured, with an uninterrupted weave of religious symbolism. The title derives from a passage in the Bible which foretells that when the violent capture the kingdom of heaven from the righteous, it is a sign of the coming of the Messiah.

When it was published in 1960, O'Connor's second novel received impressive reviews that greatly added to her growing status as a writer. To critics who called her use of violence excessive, O'Connor defended herself: "When I write a novel in which the central action is a baptism, I am very well aware that for a majority of my readers, baptism is a meaningless rite, and so in my novel I have to see that this baptism carries enough awe and mystery to jar the reader into some kind of emotional recognition of its significance." Her distortion, she said, was meant to reveal, not destroy.

In the early 1960s, O'Connor worked steadily on stories she hoped to collect in another volume. Though the civil rights movement was sweeping the South, in her fiction the author dealt indirectly with integration, which she saw as an external, social solution to problems that had their roots in the spirit. In her title story, "Everything That Rises Must Converge," she sets up a confrontation between an ignorant but charming old lady representing the South's old order and her wastrel son representing the new, but the focus quickly shifts to a higher level. The son's pride and egotism in co-opting the struggles of blacks is quickly revealed, with tragic results.

In story after story, those who reject the spiritual and embrace the secular meet with disaster. In "The Lame Shall Enter First," psychoanalysis is shown to be inadequate to handle the problems of two troubled youths; the suicide of one of them is the result. In "Greenleaf," which won a first-place O. Henry award in 1957, a widowed dairy farmer is "a good Christian woman with a large respect for religion, though she did not, of course, believe any of it was true." Her comeuppance comes via a goring by a bull. In "Revelation," a smug woman who daily thanks Jesus for not creating her a "nigger" or "white trash" is enlightened when, after being physically attacked and declared "a wart hog from hell" by a mad young woman, she experiences a vision:

> . . . a vast horde of souls were rumbling toward heaven. There were whole companies of white-trash, clean for the first time in their lives, and bands of black niggers in white robes, and battalions of freaks and lunatics shouting and clapping and leaping like frogs. And

bringing up the end of the procession was a tribe of people whom she recognized at once as those . . . like herself . . . she could see by their shocked and altered faces that even their virtues were being burned away.

In 1962, O'Connor was awarded an honorary doctorate by St. Mary's College of Notre Dame University, and the following year the same honor was accorded by Smith College. The author had been living in relatively good health when, early in 1964, she was hospitalized for the removal of an abdominal tumor. Though the growth was benign, the operation set off a flare-up of her lupus, and her health went into its final decline. Knowing she was dying, the author struggled to complete the stories that would make up her second collection. One of the last stories she completed, "Judgment Day," is a more compassionate reworking of her first published story, "The Geranium," and deals with the issue of mortality the author herself was facing, and with resurrection, in which she fervently believed.

In the summer of 1964, O'Connor fell into a coma, and she died at age thirty-nine on August 3, 1964. Her friends the Fitzgeralds believed that she had completed nearly all of the work she had set out to do. Her last story collection was published the following year.

Flannery O'Connor's literary reputation, along with critical interest and analysis of her work, has been growing ever since her death. The lectures she gave on writing, as well as other published pieces of nonfiction, were collected in *Mystery and Manners: Occasional Prose*, published posthumously in 1969. When her collected stories were published in one volume in 1971, the book won the National Book Award. Her letters, edited by her friend Sally Fitzgerald, were published in 1979 under the title *The Habit of Being*.

O'Connor is noted for using violence in her writing as a symptom of a desperate world, hungry for Christianity. The grotesque characters and happenings in her stories are both comic and tragic, revealing the sublime behind the ugly surfaces of life. Yet the author would always insist that her use of the grotesque was a true representation, rather than a distortion of reality. She portrayed ordinary people, she said, in their "fallen state." Other practitioners in this school of "Southern Grotesque" or "Gothic" include William Faulkner and Eudora Welty, who preceded her, and her contemporaries Carson McCullers, Truman Capote, and Tennessee Williams.

Like other writers in the southern agrarian tradition such as Erskine Caldwell, Allen Tate, and Robert Penn Warren, she deplored the "new South"'s urbanization and its rejection of its Bible-based roots. But unlike these authors, who cherished the southern grace and traditions of pre–Civil War times, O'Connor's fiction pointed invariably toward the grace that only God could provide. Concern with the supernatural meaning of all human life pervades her fiction.

When O'Connor's first story collection came out, the English novelist Evelyn Waugh dubiously commented in his review, "If this is the unaided work of a young lady it is a remarkable product."

O'Connor herself never considered her own work unaided. She felt that she had been given a gift for a purpose—that writers were prophets—and she never strayed from the divine vision that directed her life and art.

Chronology

March 25, 1925	born in Savannah, Georgia
1938	moves with family to Milledgeville, Georgia, after father is stricken with lupus
1942–45	attends Georgia State College for Women
1945	awarded Rinehart fellowship to study creative writing at the University of Iowa
1946	publishes first story, "The Geranium," in *Accent*; wins Rinehart Iowa Prize for a first novel
1947	receives master of fine arts degree from University of Iowa
1948	stays at Yaddo, in Saratoga Springs, New York
1949	lives with Robert and Sally Fitzgerald in Ridgefield, Connecticut
1950	becomes ill with lupus; moves home to Milledgeville
1952	first novel, *Wise Blood*, published
1953	awarded *Kenyon Review* fellowship
1954	*Kenyon Review* fellowship renewed; wins second-place O. Henry award for "The Life You Save May Be Your Own"
1955	first story collection, *A Good Man Is Hard to Find*, published; wins second-place O. Henry award for "A Circle in the Fire"
1956	travels and lectures at colleges and universities

1957	awarded grant from National Institute of Arts and Letters; wins first-place O. Henry award for "Greenleaf"
1958	travels to Lourdes and Rome with mother, has audience with pope
1959	receives Ford Foundation grant
1960	second novel, *The Violent Bear It Away*, published
August 3, 1964	dies in Milledgeville

Further Reading

O'Connor's Works

The Complete Stories of Flannery O'Connor. New York: Farrar, Straus & Giroux, 1971. The author's stories collected, in roughly chronological order, with an introduction by her friend Robert Giroux.

Three by Flannery O'Connor. New York: Penguin, 1983. The author's two novels along with her second short-story collection in one volume, with a biographical introduction by Sally Fitzgerald.

Books About O'Connor

Grimshaw, James A., Jr. *The Flannery O'Connor Companion.* Westport, Conn.: Greenwood, 1981. Literary guide that will help readers understand the rich symbolism of the author's works.

Index

Boldface headings and page numbers indicate main topics. Italic page numbers indicate illustrations or captions. Page numbers followed by c indicate chronology.

Index

Index

Index

Index

Index